The Sarbanes-Oxley Debacle

AEI LIABILITY STUDIES
Michael S. Greve
Series Editor

The AEI Liability Studies examine aspects of the U.S. civil liability system central to the political debates over liability reform. Individual studies analyze the consequences of important liability doctrines for consumer welfare and productive efficiency, assess the effectiveness of recently enacted liability reforms, examine intricate jurisdictional and institutional dilemmas, and propound original proposals for improvement. The goal of the series is to contribute new empirical evidence and promising reform ideas that are commensurate to the seriousness of America's liability problems.

TWO CHEERS FOR CONTINGENT FEES
*Alexander Tabarrok and
Eric Helland*

HARM-LESS LAWSUITS?
WHAT'S WRONG WITH CONSUMER CLASS ACTIONS
Michael S. Greve

The Sarbanes-Oxley Debacle

What We've Learned; How to Fix It

Henry N. Butler and Larry E. Ribstein

The AEI Press

Publisher for the American Enterprise Institute

WASHINGTON, D.C.

2006

Distributed to the Trade by National Book Network, 15200 NBN Way, Blue Ridge Summit, PA 17214. To order call toll free 1-800-462-6420 or 1-717-794-3800. For all other inquiries please contact the AEI Press, 1150 Seventeenth Street, N.W., Washington, D.C. 20036 or call 1-800-862-5801.

Library of Congress Cataloging-in-Publication Data
Butler, Henry N.
   The Sarbanes-Oxley debacle: what we've learned; how to fix it /
Henry N. Butler and Larry E. Ribstein.
      p. cm.
Includes index.
   ISBN-13: 978-0-8447-7194-6 (pbk : alk. paper)
   ISBN-10: 0-8447-7194-5
   1. Corporations—Auditing—Law and legislation—United States.
   2. Financial disclosure—Law and legislation—United States.
   3. Corporate governance—Law and legislation—United States.
   4. Securities fraud—United States—Prevention. 5. United States.
Sarbanes-Oxley Act of 2002. I. Ribstein, Larry E. II. Title.

   KF1446.B88 2006
   346.73'0666—dc22

2006013205

11 10 09 08 07 06   1 2 3 4 5 6

Printed in the United States of America

Contents

Foreword

The "liability explosion" would be much easier to address if it were in fact, as the term implies, a sudden event with a specific cause. But the expansion of legal liability beyond its traditional common-law boundaries has been a gradual, evolutionary process, with numerous interwoven causes. For example, until a century ago tort cases were, for the most part, disputes between citizens of the same political jurisdiction, decided by local judges and juries. With the emergence of large corporations and the growth of interstate commerce, tort cases increasingly pitted local plaintiffs against out-of-state citizens or corporations with highly diffused ownership—but were still decided by judges and juries of the plaintiffs' states or communities, whose tendency to dispense justice with more attentive sympathy for neighbor-plaintiffs than for foreigner-defendants was strong and systematic. Beneficial economic developments produced an unfortunate byproduct: the transformation of a system of dispute resolution into the unconstrained imposition of a tort tax.

The progressive expansion of liability had many political, intellectual, and even cultural causes in addition to economic ones. Although many changes in legal doctrines and procedures were reasonable adaptations to social change, by the end of the twentieth century the system as a whole was producing many results that were manifestly unjust, socially harmful, and economically counterproductive. Still, the movement for legal reform was as slow and complex as the phenomena it responded to. Not only had free-wheeling liability produced a politically powerful interest group adamantly opposed to reform—the trial lawyers—but the liability system itself was highly decentralized, with many subtle features and interdependent parts. Many proposals to improve it by revising one or another legal rule foundered on the problem of top-down regulation: Revising a single feature of a complex system leads the other features to respond in kind, which may leave matters even worse than they were before. Only in recent years, a quarter-century after the liability explosion first attracted political notice, have state and federal reforms begun to appear with serious evidence or prospects of yielding tangible improvements.

The problems of excessive legal liability have been a longstanding concern of the American Enterprise Institute. In this monograph series, AEI aims to inform the growing political debates with original, intellectually rigorous research and scholarship by some of America's leading students of law and economics. Series editor Michael S. Greve, who is John G. Searle Scholar at AEI, is himself a leading thinker and writer as well as an activist in liability-reform circles. The studies presented here aim to be attuned to the strengths as well as deficiencies of our civil liability system, and to address the most serious issues in the policy debates. Some contributions supply much-needed empirical data and analysis, while others tackle the intricate institutional problems of the civil justice system. Above all, the studies aim to contribute fresh ideas and practical reform proposals that are commensurate to the depth and gravity of the problem of unbounded liability.

CHRISTOPHER DEMUTH
President
American Enterprise Institute
for Public Policy Research

Introduction

The Sarbanes-Oxley Act of 2002 (SOX) emerged from the spectacular crashes of Enron, WorldCom, and other corporations after the bursting of the dot.com stock market bubble. Enron and WorldCom became poster children for the supposed "separation of ownership and control" problems first publicized seventy years earlier by Adolf Berle and Gardiner Means and echoed by generations of corporate scholars ever since.[1] After the millennial frauds, the usual proponents of reform argued for regulation that would restore "investor confidence" in the securities markets. Congress responded with the most sweeping federal securities legislation since the original laws in 1933 and 1934.

Since 2003, the direct costs of SOX have become evident. Despite, or perhaps because of, the significant indications of costs and problems related to SOX, many journalists in prominent magazines have rushed to the act's defense in its fourth year of life.[2] Their argument goes something like this: There was fraud; SOX was designed to reduce fraud by requiring more honesty and disclosure; therefore, SOX is good. For example, The New Yorker's James Surowiecki acknowledges SOX's significant costs, but emphasizes the social costs of fraud—that WorldCom made its rivals look less efficient than they were, resulting in misallocation of resources. Joe Nocera of the New York Times stresses that accountants now have a regulator, the U.S. Securities and Exchange Commission (SEC) has more money, CEOs must vouch for their firms' financial statements, corporate loans are outlawed, directors must be more independent, and the internal controls disclosures are revealing useful information.[3] Nocera also acknowledges the expenses under SOX, but says the costs are starting to drop, and that the SEC is working to reduce the burden on smaller companies. *Business Week* has blithely asserted that SOX "is enabling businesses to cut costs and boosts productivity." Perhaps Congress should apply its managerial prowess more broadly.[4]

Praise for SOX is also pouring in from those who participated in its creation. Representative Michael Oxley, who shepherded the House version of SOX and provided its surname, says, "The system is much better now. . . . We have come a long way since the economic dark days that are only a couple of years behind us." Investors once were "losing confidence in the American markets." Now, he says,

> boards are working harder, playing more of the role that they were designed for. They are responding to shareholders and increasing dividends and buybacks. Audit committees are more active and more independent. They are using their authority to engage independent counsel. The PCAOB [Public Company Accounting Oversight Board] is up and running and is actively reviewing auditing firms.[5]

As a result, he says, corporate profits, jobs, stock prices, venture capital, and research and development spending are up, and bankruptcies are down. In other words, Oxley attributes to SOX the turn in the business cycle. Next, like Lear, he will be crediting it with atmospheric phenomena. While it is understandable that Oxley would overstate the benefits of his namesake, one should be skeptical of his self-serving assessment.

Former SEC chairman Arthur Levitt, a key proponent of several of SOX's provisions, wrote in the *Wall Street Journal* to oppose SOX exemptions for small public firms proposed in December by an SEC advisory committee.[6] Levitt insists, remarkably, that "the small-business lobby" is seeking changes that "would make it more difficult for smaller companies to attract capital needed for growth and undermine confidence in the markets." In other words, he is so sure of the wisdom of the changes he helped adopt that he is willing to assume that the "small-business lobby" is lobbying against its own interests. Levitt ignores the fact that this supposedly powerful lobby was too weak to prevent passage of the act.[7] Moreover, it is hard to accept that exempting firms constituting only 7 percent of the capitalization of the market would undermine investor confidence in the entire market.

No one can deny that there have been some benefits from SOX, including the increased information revealed by the internal controls disclosures. Moreover, the business world is clearly performing better now than in the chaotic days before SOX. The relevant policy questions are whether the benefits exceed the costs, and whether the business world is better now *because* of SOX.

While proponents in Congress and the media have been creative in finding social benefits deriving from SOX, they have not been equally thorough in understanding its full costs. SOX defenders focus on direct costs, such as increased audit fees. But while these are substantial (approximately $6 billion per year), they are only the tip of the iceberg—with much larger but less obvious costs accruing beneath the surface. Indeed, the best evidence indicates that SOX imposes additional net losses of $1.1 trillion. This monograph demonstrates that its supporters are utterly misguided in their assessment: Both logic and evidence make it clear that SOX was a costly mistake.

As we will discuss in chapter 1, SOX's problems are unsurprising, given the circumstances of its birth. Enron may or may not have helped set off a market panic, but what ensued was clearly a Code Red regulatory panic. When one combines the efforts of proregulatory interest groups with the avid news media reports of corporate fraud, it is not surprising either that SOX was enacted, or that it still has many defenders. Although there were significant ambiguities about precisely what, if any, problems needed fixing, Congress was in no mood for ambiguities. The prevailing regulatory philosophy was "shoot first and ask questions later." We are only now asking the right questions and getting the correct, if depressing, answers.

Chapter 2 provides a good starting point for asking these questions by considering what investors—the putative beneficiaries of SOX—desire in antifraud regulations. Clearly, investors do not like to be defrauded. To the extent government regulation can prevent fraud, shareholders benefit. But shareholders will find such regulation valuable only if the benefit from reduced fraud is greater than the cost of regulatory compliance. SOX's attempt to create a perfect world with zero fraud goes too far. Moreover, it is well-accepted in the financial economics literature that the costs and benefits of securities regulation should be evaluated from the perspective of typical shareholders who can avoid some costs of fraud by investing in diversified portfolios of shares. By imposing the costs of eliminating fraud on all firms in investors' portfolios, the SOX mandates are a terrible deal for the ordinary investors it purports to protect.

Although the act's defenders assert that the business world is better off now than before SOX, chapter 3 makes it clear that the relevant question is whether the business world is better *because* of SOX. The American corporate governance system is incredibly dynamic—for over a hundred years, it has demonstrated its resilience and ability to evolve in response to dramatic structural changes and external shocks. Even if there were a problem that needed solving, it is likely that existing institutions and the market could have solved it without a massive new dose of one-size-fits-all regulation from the federal government. Moreover, given the dynamism and success of our system, the proponents of massive new regulation logically should bear the burden of justifying it. To frame the question of whether SOX was necessary, we consider what would have happened if there had been no SOX. American markets would not simply have turned into a costly casino with careful investors stuffing their money in mattresses. Existing market devices and regulation have already worked to punish the pre-SOX frauds and, thus, to deter future fraud. If new rules had been necessary, capital-hungry companies, stock exchanges, states, and professional groups would have had ample incentive to provide them, and thereby to demonstrate their integrity to investors. They also had better information than politicians and regulators about what to do. It is highly unlikely that Congress could outthink this dynamic system, particularly during the frenzied regulatory panic of 2002.

The costs of SOX are described in chapters 4 and 5. In general, defenders have limited their calculations to the act's most direct compliance costs. They, like Congress in 2002, ignore indirect and possibly hidden—but still quite substantial—costs. Chapter 4 surveys the mounting evidence on the direct costs of SOX—particularly those of complying with the notorious section 404 internal controls—that have triggered so much interest in the media, and then discusses in detail some of the less obvious costs, including interference with business management, distraction of managers, risk aversion by independent directors, over-criminalization of agency costs, reduced access to capital markets, and the crippling of the dynamic federalism that has created the best corporate governance structure in the world.

Chapter 5 describes the ticking litigation time bomb SOX has created. The first major market correction will be painful for investors, but it will be a gigantic litigation festival for trial lawyers. SOX gives litigators the benefit of 20/20 hindsight to identify minor or technical reporting mistakes as the basis for lawsuits against corporations, officers, and directors. The threat of litigation on this scale should in no way be construed as investor protection.

Chapter 6 compares the small benefits of SOX discussed in chapter 3 with the large costs discussed in chapters 4 and 5. Based upon the best available evidence, it concludes that SOX has imposed a net loss on the American economy of $1.4 trillion. A widely cited study of the annual direct costs of complying with SOX indicates that firms will spend a total of $6 billion in 2006.[8] Even if annual direct costs of this magnitude were going to continue in perpetuity, the present value of those costs would amount to only a small fraction of $1.4 trillion net loss. A conservative estimate is that the indirect costs of SOX are greater than $1.1 trillion.[9]

Chapter 7 considers the potential policy implications of our conclusion that SOX is a colossal mistake. A favorable court decision in a recently filed lawsuit could provide the leverage to enact some major changes in SOX. On February 8, 2006, the Free Enterprise Fund filed a lawsuit alleging that the accounting oversight board SOX created violates the appointments clause of the Constitution because its members should be appointed by the president or heads of executive branch departments rather than by the SEC.[10] This suit has the potential to overturn all of SOX, which lacks a severability clause. However, if the Free Enterprise Fund prevails, the courts are likely to give Congress a window of opportunity to fix it. Although political reality makes it unlikely that Congress will repeal SOX, it may have the incentive to respond to the increasing criticism of SOX and fix its most egregious flaws.

Several relatively minor changes in the statute could greatly reduce the burden that SOX imposes on the American economy. First, SOX should be amended to prohibit private lawsuits. Second, it should be amended to exempt securities of foreign corporations. Third, it should be amended to exempt all but the largest corporations. Fourth, it should be amended to allow shareholder opt-out of at least some provisions through shareholder proxy proposals. Finally, the criminal sanctions in SOX should be removed.

Chapter 8 takes a longer view. The post-SOX era offers real opportunities to assess what we have learned about policymaking from the Sarbanes-Oxley fiasco. Given policymakers' tendency to overreact in market panics, doubts about the efficacy and costs of federal regulation, and the availability of other mechanisms for controlling corporate fraud, there is much to be said for a careful approach to federal regulation that, among other things, allows for alternatives and limits the scope of regulation. Perhaps something can be salvaged from the SOX fiasco.

1

From Enron to SOX: Shoot First,
Ask Questions Later

An assessment of SOX should begin with its passage. What did we know about the costs and benefits of regulation, and when did we know it? If Congress had known that the costs of SOX were going to be as high as they turned out to be, would it nonetheless have passed the act? This chapter shows that Congress knew very little when it acted precipitously, in the midst of a regulatory panic. An understanding of the defects of this process may help us prevent a similar mistake the next time the conditions are ripe for such a panic.

Enron

The long millennial bull market, which had peaked in March 2000, dropped even before September 11, 2001. By late September, trillions in shareholder wealth had evaporated. So the market was in an ugly mood when Enron Corporation disclosed on October 16, 2001, that it was taking a half-billion-dollar after-tax charge against earnings and a $1.2 billion reduction of shareholders' equity because it was revising its accounting for transactions with one of its so-called "special-purpose entities." Thus began Enron's collapse into litigation and bankruptcy.

It was a spectacular fall. Enron had been a model for the new economy, pioneering a way to create markets that heralded drastically reduced transaction costs. Enron showed, for example, that utility companies did not have to own energy sources to ensure fuel sources—they could buy the energy through Enron's energy market.

Fortune had ranked Enron the most innovative company in America for six straight years, and its chief executive, Jeff Skilling, now known mainly as a criminal defendant, had been named the nation's second-best executive (after Microsoft's Steve Ballmer) as recently as six months before the collapse. Business school classes had admired Enron's business model. After October, 2001, they rapidly turned to studying Enron as a classic example of business failure.[1]

As first detailed in the so-called Powers Report, issued in February 2002, Enron executives had created earnings for the company and its insiders by disguising speculation as hedging, making murky deals with hazy special-purpose entities, and claiming as revenues predictions of years of sales and prepayments on commodities contracts.[2] The report spread the blame widely. Senior officers were either involved in the transactions or oddly ignorant of what was going on. The Enron board, including its fully independent audit committee, knew of problems, but it put its faith in representations by senior officers that they would police the insider deals and in assurances by the company's accounting firm, Arthur Andersen. Andersen, in turn, and its partner in charge of the Enron account, failed adequately to scrutinize their major customer of both audit and nonaudit services. Meanwhile, despite indications that all was not well at Enron, securities analysts continued to give buy recommendations, and the major debt-rating agencies rated Enron's debt as investment grade until shortly before the crash.

The Post-Enron Regulatory Panic. Something had happened to Enron, but it was not clear what. Clearly some corporate executives had been dishonest, but they were being found out and punished under existing law. Companies already had plenty of watchdogs. Enron and WorldCom had independent directors and auditors. Securities analysts seemingly had ample incentives to watch them closely.

As detailed in Roberta Romano's exhaustive study of SOX's legislative history, Congress acted precipitously, without anything resembling a balanced consideration of the issues.[3] The House passed a relatively mild bill in April 2002, after the stock market had recovered somewhat and the public had become calmer. It focused on increased criminal penalties to exact the vengeance against executives the public was demanding, and provided for an accounting industry watchdog. However, by the end of July the Senate had passed, and the House and Senate had agreed to in conference, a much stricter law. The Senate version included several more consequential corporate governance measures, among them a prohibition on executive loans, and requirements of audit committee independence and executive certification of financial statements. This bill was reported out of the conference committee on July 23 and quickly passed and signed into law July 30, 2002, by President George W. Bush, who described the law as putting into effect "the most far-reaching reforms of American business practices since the time of Franklin Delano Roosevelt."[4]

What happened to propel this law from a modest bill to a far-reaching law through a divided Congress in only three months? The answer to this question reveals much about the source of the problems discussed in this monograph. The following are some of the relevant factors. Many are interrelated. Some grew out of unique events in 2002, while others reflect long-term historical trends. The main question is what they tell us about how we might avoid future SOXes.

Mounting Reports of Corporate Wrongdoing. Between April and July there were reports of numerous additional cases of corporate fraud or bad accounting. Xerox had improperly accelerated revenues from long-term equipment leases, Qwest and Global Crossing had manipulated revenues and expenses on fiber optic deals, cable firm Adelphia had apparently been looted by its controlling shareholders, and there were reports of excessive spending by Tyco CEO Dennis Kozlowski. Most spectacularly of all, WorldCom collapsed into bankruptcy after disclosing that it had falsely claimed as assets billions of dollars it had paid as ordinary business expenses to use its transmission networks.

But what did all this mean? The media suggested that all of it was connected, and that it indicated a drastic increase in the total amount of fraud. Was this was the reality? Were the stories actually connected in a way that called for coherent government action? Looting by executives is a different problem from accounting errors, not least because the former is already well-covered by existing law. Moreover, connecting looting, a real problem, with accounting errors, may tend to make the latter look worse than it is.

The Stock Market Decline. The stock market had been declining since early March 2002—possibly as the direct result of investor concerns over the growing threat of war in Iraq. This decline created political pressure to do something about mounting corporate fraud in order to "restore confidence" in the market.[5] The market reached a temporary low in late July, around the time of the vote on the conference committee bill. In fact, the Dow Jones Industrial Average dropped a thousand points in July alone. Just as investors' judgment errors may have played a role in the run-up in stock prices prior to 2001, so they may have figured in the post-boom panic. Ironically, SOX itself may have been responsible for that decline, since stock prices plunged around the time that it became evident Congress would pass a stringent version of SOX.[6]

The News Media's Role. During the first half of 2002 the news media were unrelentingly negative on business: 77 percent of the 613 major network evening news stories between January and July concerned corporate scandals, of which 195 connected corporations to Congress and 188 to the Bush administration, compared to 11 percent of 489 business stories about scandals in the same period the prior year.

This suggests that corporate crime was quite salient in the public mind during deliberations on SOX.[7] Salience tends to drive the political agenda; people think more about corporate crime than about the potential costs of laws intended to deal with it. Moreover, the news media undoubtedly play a role in creating this salience by deciding which stories are featured prominently, and how they are portrayed.

Because the media are obviously important players in the political process, it is important to examine their incentives. Evidence indicates that news media bias toward the left produces more regulation.[8] Moreover, noted financial economist Michael Jensen has characterized the press as producers of entertainment rather than information. Jensen says that readers want simple answers delivered in an entertaining way.[9] This suggests that the press will tend to exaggerate market excesses colorfully and support simple regulatory solutions that ignore the complexity of the underlying problems. To be sure, readers also demand correct information. But a recent study testing these alternative hypotheses shows significant evidence of sensationalism in coverage of executive compensation.[10]

Applying these insights to SOX, it is clear that the millennial stock market crash created a market for entertaining stories about bad businesspeople. The media saw gains in a continuing saga of corporate fraud that readers or viewers would follow avidly day by day. This conveniently meshed with the media's proregulatory bias. All of this negative coverage interacted with the public's anxiety about the economy and the market, its tendency to stress recent prominent news, and general populist sentiments about business, discussed further below.

The Lack of Effective Political Opposition by Probusiness Interests. Several factors usually serve as inherent brakes on enactment of business legislation, particularly laws as sweeping and multifarious as SOX. While there are always reformers and business groups in favor of regulation that may be socially harmful, for instance, the social costs are often felt by firms and interest groups who are in a position to bear the costs of lobbying against the reform effort.[11] The political process provides ample opportunity for firms and groups to express and organize opposition and slow down legislation. Laws like SOX must wend their way through both houses of Congress, beginning in committee and finally working their way to the floor. Even if a single party dominates both houses, this apparent unity may mask significant disagreement among the relevant business groups. That is particularly so with most business legislation, which rarely pushes galvanizing hot buttons.

In the case of SOX, the houses were controlled by different parties—Republicans had the House, while Democrats had the Senate. This created the conditions for disagreement not only within parties and within legislative bodies, but between the houses of Congress. We have already noted that, true to the differing party alignments, the House initially passed a significantly weaker version of the law that became SOX than did the Senate. Yet it was the Senate's version that eventually became law, and quickly at that. Why did the usual "brakes" of interest groups and the political process apparently fail here? One possible reason, of course, is that the conditions outlined above, as well as others still to be discussed, created significant public pressure for action. Another is that the Bush administration needed to demonstrate its disapproval of its former political ally, Kenneth Lay of Enron, who was now a notorious symbol of corporate malfeasance.

Despite these politics, business groups might have stopped the SOX juggernaut if they had been united.[12] The U.S. Chamber of Commerce did give battle. Its members included smaller firms that were more sensitive to sharp increases in monitoring costs, were not susceptible to blame for the most public corporate frauds, and did not have to worry as much about a backlash from public shareholders or customers who might be incensed by their opposition to corporate reform. The Business Roundtable did not, however, oppose SOX. It represented big business, which in the summer of 2002 was concerned less about regulatory costs than about avoiding the public's ire. These companies might have concluded that supporting the government's moves against fraud would provide them with cheap public relations—or at least that it would be costly in terms of public relations to oppose them. Moreover, no one seemed to be representing the interests of foreign issuers, not even the U.S. securities industry that derived significant revenues from trading these shares. And, of course, there was no one to defend the interests of potential future firms stillborn because of high regulatory costs.

There were deeper reasons business interests supported SOX even after its high costs became apparent. Firms might have been particularly willing to support legislation that imposed regulatory costs if those that bore the most costs were their competitors. For example, Henry Manne argued that the original federal securities laws helped leading securities firms that underwrote relatively low-risk, high-disclosure securities to compete against firms that served a higher-risk clientele.[13] With respect to the costs of SOX, it was significant that bigger companies might have smaller rivals. The biggest worry for all big companies was the next big thing, which would come bubbling up from the venture capital incubator— unless SOX prevented it.

Some of the more vocal business supporters of SOX were the accountants and others in the monitoring and consulting industry who audit, investigate, prosecute and defend fraud, as well as prepare disclosure documents.[14] It is ironic that some of the biggest winners from SOX have been those whose gatekeeping failures triggered the law in the first place. Joseph Nocera of the *New York Times* views this as

> one of the unintended consequences—that Sarbanes-Oxley has been a financial boon to the profession, since all the big accounting firms have to audit a company's financial controls as well as its books. "In effect, the law is giving the auditors business," Senator Sarbanes said with a chuckle. But so what? Better that they make money doing actual auditing work than by selling themselves as consultants.[15]

Public choice economics suggests, however, that the intent of SOX should be inferred from its consequences. In this view, the accounting lobby—who Nocera says was the "primary opponent of Sarbanes-Oxley"—was pleased with the passage of SOX.[16] As Yale law professor Jonathan Macey has said,

> The politicalization of the process of corporate governance has produced massively perverse results. Specifically, those corporate governance institutions

> that have performed the worst have been rewarded,
> while those institutions that have performed the best
> have been hampered by legal rules designed to impede
> the ability to operate. Rather than producing genuine
> reform, the wave of corporate governance, accounting
> and capital markets scandals of the 1990s have gener-
> ated political responses that benefit narrow interest
> groups and harm investors. Politics, not economics,
> determines which corporate governance devices are
> favored and which are not. As a consequence, the most
> effective corporate governance devices tend to be dis-
> favored, while the ineffective mechanisms are rewarded
> in the regulatory process.[17]

Some firms may have supported SOX because it appeased public passion for reform as cheaply as possible. Indeed, firms may
continue to believe that the act's main importance is symbolic.
Roberta Romano notes that this may explain the increased criminal
sanctions, at least, as indicated by the extent to which these were
emphasized by legislators in their debates and by opinion polls on
the public's view of SOX.[18] But this does not account for the act's
governance reforms, which were not featured in the debates.
Romano believes the symbolism explanation is inconsistent with
the high actual costs of governance reforms.

The failure of business to stop the SOX juggernaut also owes
something to the Republicans, who normally could be expected to
defend business interests. Although the Republicans did slow
down the train in the House in April, by the summer they could no
longer provide effective opposition. Facing midterm elections in
November, the party controlling the White House and identified
with business stood to lose much more than the Democrats as the
result of any public ire about the economy and corporate misconduct. Corporate fraud helped the Democrats discredit Republican
deregulatory and antitax policies. Republicans therefore risked
damaging their agenda by siding with opponents of regulation. The
choice between keeping or increasing control and temporarily

abandoning some of their constituents might have seemed easy, particularly since those constituents were divided and had their own reasons for wanting the Republicans in power.

Moreover, the Republicans had a more significant problem. On July 4, the press had revived a story from twelve years earlier about President Bush's failure to file an appropriate notice of his 1990 sale of the stock of Harken Energy while he was a director of that company.[19] Bush held a news conference on July 8, looking like he had been caught with his hand in the cookie jar. The next day he announced a set of corporate governance reforms, including executive certification of financial statements, stiffer criminal sentences, and restrictions on nonaudit services by accounting firms. The reforms also condemned insider loans, though the president did not suggest dealing with them by federal or other law.

The political picture was therefore darkening rapidly for the Republicans. They needed corporate reform legislation quickly, or at least could not afford to be seen as obstructing it. This helps explain why they consented to a cloture motion in the Senate.[20] Cloture effectively prevented amendments on the Senate floor, the main exception being Senator Charles E. Schumer's executive loan provision, discussed below.

The Republicans still might have hoped to avoid a disastrous law through negotiations in conference. But things rapidly got worse for them when, on July 10, a story appeared about the president's below-market-rate loan from Harken, also while he was a director.[21] By July 11, the story was all over the media.[22] Again, politics was shaped by a combination of actual events and deliberate news media decisions concerning what stories to feature—in this case, a decision to investigate President Bush's twelve-year-old conduct in the business world just as other corporate fraud stories were emerging.

So, as the Senate and House proceeded to conference July 16 over their very different versions of corporate reform—a conference in which Republicans had hoped to modify the more drastic Senate version of the act that had emerged from the cloture vote—the Republicans were in a political corner. The president pressured the House Republicans for a quick compromise with the Senate, saying that "the two [chambers] need to get together as quickly as possible and get me a bill that I can sign before the August recess."[23] Among Republicans there was "a mad dash to embrace the Sarbanes bill,"[24] which left lobbyists little room to make last-minute adjustments. By July 25, 2002, the deal had been made, and the consensus bill passed the House 422-3 and the Senate 99-0.

The Role of Policy Entrepreneurs. Roberta Romano stresses the role of "policy entrepreneurs" in shaping SOX provisions on executive loans, independent audit committees, executive certification of financial statements, and provision of nonaudit services.[25] These influential participants in Congress's deliberations saw a new opportunity to press proposals they had long favored without success. While the witnesses may have been sincere, the one-sidedness of their testimony clearly contributed to Congress's flawed policymaking.

For example, in the Senate committee hearings on the bill that became SOX, former SEC chairman Arthur Levitt Jr. and chief accountant Lynn Turner pushed their agendas on independent audit committees and restrictions on nonaudit services by auditors. The latter was an initiative Levitt had pushed two years earlier, only to be defeated by the efforts of Harvey Pitt on behalf of the big auditing firms. At the time of the SOX deliberations, Pitt was the SEC chairman, but he was unpopular among congressional Democrats. Other policy entrepreneurs who testified in the Senate included corporate lawyer and prominent governance reform advocate Ira Milstein, who advocated fully independent audit committees. The witness list in the Senate was shaped by the proregulatory committee chair, Senator Paul Sarbanes.

As proreform witnesses ignored evidence of which they were aware, doubt was cast on the wisdom and effectiveness of these proposals. For example, Romano recounts the testimony of witnesses, including Levitt, on the need to restrict auditors from providing nonaudit services. The witnesses failed to mention that the Panel on Audit Effectiveness, whose creation Levitt himself had suggested, had found no evidence that the performance of nonaudit services had actually impaired audit quality.[26] Referring to the report in 2000 of this panel and to a 1978 report reaching the same conclusion, Romano says,

> It should be noted that . . . witnesses who advocated a prohibition, such as Levitt, were, without question, fully aware of both reports, but one would not have known that from their testimony. The lack of candor is embarrassing.[27]

One wonders how Levitt would have treated a comparable lack of candor in SEC disclosure documents.

The opinions expressed at the committee hearings by prominent policy entrepreneurs resonated with the views of academic reformers who, since the 1930s, had urged increased federal regulation of corporate governance. Moreover, they meshed with the interests of trial lawyers, who had chafed against the restrictions on securities class remedies and lawsuits that were in the Private Securities Litigation Reform Act of 1995 (PSLRA) and imposed by the Supreme Court. In particular, the trial lawyers supported Senator Patrick Leahy's effort to lengthen the statute of limitations on securities actions. This gave Democrats a negotiating tool to get the Republicans to agree to cloture.[28] Since lawyers, particularly transactional lawyers who advised on corporate governance, had an interest in tightening governance requirements, an American Bar Association task force representing their interests made recommendations dealing not only with lawyers but with corporate governance generally, including an endorsement of increased director independence.[29]

The question is what influence these policy entrepreneurs may have had on the final legislation. Romano points out that the corporate governance proposals they championed could not be dismissed as symbolic politics—that is, something to wave in front of a gullible public to show that the politicians were doing something.[30] In fact, the politicians did not do much waving—the proposals were hardly discussed in floor debates. These were the sort of "inside-the-beltway" proposals about which the general public cares little, particularly compared with more salient issues like increased criminal penalties for misconduct, which everybody can understand.

The role of the policy entrepreneurs may have been to provide grist for the political mill. Although the political environment may have been conducive to regulation, politicians need specific proposals to enact. The policy entrepreneurs put their weight behind some. The proposals may not have been symbols in themselves, but they at least served to lend substance to the final legislation—in itself a potent symbol that Congress had done something about corporate malfeasance.

The result of the hodgepodge of proposals that came out of the woodwork was legislation that extended far beyond the problems that triggered the regulatory panic, including strict new regulation of the auditor-client relationship and the imposition of a large additional bureaucracy on the accounting profession.

Populism and Political Entrepreneurs. Like other products, legislation needs to be sold to its consumers—in this case, the voters. Legislators sometimes have a special ability to match opportunistically specific legislative proposals with the public mood. Jayne Barnard has detailed how Senator Schumer was able to do this with respect to what may be one of the most intrusive and costly SOX provisions—the outlawing of certain loans to insiders.[31]

As discussed above, President Bush's political problems over his Harken loans were an important factor in putting pressure on Republicans to support SOX. More specifically, Bush had decried executive loans in a July 9 speech shortly after the first Harken story, which Schumer had attended, though he had not proposed any legislation to deal with them. The *Wall Street Journal* nevertheless noted that day that the loans were "too popular to disappear anytime soon."[32]

"Soon" had a special meaning in this fast-moving political context. When Bush's own inside loan was reported shortly thereafter, Schumer realized that the time was ripe for a move. So, on July 12,

2002, after obtaining White House support, he introduced an amendment in the Senate outlawing insider loans. This was one of only three amendments that were made after cloture, and got special consideration because of Bush's Harken problem.[33] In his statements supporting the amendment, Schumer explicitly played the populism card, asking, "Why can't these super rich corporate executives go to the corner bank, the SunTrust's or Bank of America's, like everyone else to take loans?"[34] The amendment passed without discussion by voice vote.[35]

The Boom-Bust Regulatory Cycle. SOX was arguably just one example of the "Sudden Acute Regulatory Syndrome"[36] that usually follows a market panic—like the Bubble Act passed in England in the midst of the South Sea Bubble, and the federal securities laws in the United States that followed the 1929 stock market crash.[37] When the economy is booming or stable, significant new financial or corporate governance regulation will not help any particular interest group enough so that they will be willing or able to apply pressure for it—or at least enough pressure to overcome opposition by antiregulatory groups. The proregulatory groups cannot enlist the support of consumers or investors who are riding a rising market, or who are simply indifferent to a dull one.

The political dynamic changes, however, when fraud becomes a hot media story. People are susceptible to claims that regulation is needed to "restore confidence" in the market. Moreover, there is a deep-seated distrust of financial markets and an envy of rich capitalists that awakens when these markets are going down and not providing goodies. These public attitudes can be seized by policy entrepreneurs, political opportunists, and proregulatory interest groups.

This "regulatory panic" account of financial regulation suggests that laws like SOX are enacted precisely when lawmakers are least able to evaluate them properly. Lawmakers regulating in a crash are likely to underestimate the gains that a vibrant business and capital market environment can provide and ignore the regulatory costs of their actions. Such times are ripe for regulation that penalizes useful practices and generally discourages risk-taking by punishing negative results and reducing the rewards for success.

All Action, No Talk. We have shown that, for several reasons, lawmakers and voters did not seem willing to debate the costs and benefits of SOX calmly. Deliberations in Congress were sparse.[38] There was only one day of debate in the House, with hardly anyone speaking on some of the major proposals in the House bill, such as officer loans and audit committee independence. In the Senate committee, the witnesses were heavily skewed in their views of regulation, and their testimony did not attempt to balance costs and benefits, nor to present evidence that was inconsistent with their conclusions. The Senate debated the resulting bill hurriedly and under cloture, and it was passed swiftly with little revision.

Some of the factors that led to this result, such as the political environment, were specific to SOX and are unlikely to recur. But many of the factors that produce a regulatory panic have recurred over time and are likely to arise again. We are doomed to relive the SOX experience unless we can better understand the costs of this type of regulation and the excesses inherent in SOX. Congressmen and interest groups might have resisted the populism and the panic if they had better realized the havoc this type of law might cause. Since the most invasive corporate governance provisions did not, in any event, particularly resonate with the public—that is, they likely were simply pulled off the shelf to fill out the legislation—a better understanding of the costs of governance "reform" may reduce the likelihood of a future SOX. We provide those insights below.

The Sarbanes-Oxley Act

At this point it is useful to provide a quick roadmap of what Congress did in the dog days of summer 2002. The provisions will be grouped according to their general objectives.

Increased Internal Monitoring. SOX has several provisions intended to ensure better monitoring for potential fraud by a corporation's own agents. The act

- mandates that the board audit committee consist solely of independent members and be responsible for hiring and overseeing auditors;
- requires executives to certify reports, with criminal penalties for reckless certification;
- penalizes executives who fraudulently influence or mislead auditors;
- mandates disclosures concerning the firm's internal controls structure;
- mandates a code of ethics for financial officers;
- provides for protection of whistleblowers.

Gatekeeper Regulation. SOX includes provisions intended to ensure better and more disinterested performance by professionals who are supposed to scrutinize corporate transactions. The act

- requires attorney reporting of evidence of fraud;
- reduces financial ties between auditors and audited companies;
- provides for the independent Public Company Accounting Oversight Board (PCAOB).

More Disclosure. The act provides for new categories of disclosure relating to

- the firm's internal controls structure and code of ethics;
- off-balance-sheet transactions;
- pro forma earnings.

The act also provides for SEC rules requiring more rapid disclosure of material changes in financial condition.

Regulation of Insider Misconduct. Beyond disclosure and monitoring, SOX includes some direct regulation of suspect categories of insider conduct. The act

- prohibits loans to insiders;
- requires return of incentive-based compensation following accounting restatements.

Regulating Securities Analysts. The act includes provisions intended to ensure that securities analysts operate independently of their firms' investment banking activities.

2

What Shareholders Want—
The Optimal Amount of Fraud

The "separation of ownership and control"—the notion that managers of publicly traded corporations may not have incentives to act in their shareholders' best interests—has been the overriding concern of corporation law and corporate governance since before Berle and Means coined the phrase in 1932.[1] Officers and directors may take advantage of shareholders by not working hard, consuming excessive perquisites, paying themselves exorbitant salaries, hoarding cash, building empires, diversifying the corporation for their personal risk preferences, not taking enough risks, and so forth. Managers use their dominance of the director selection process to promote the election of directors who will defer to them. Shareholders let managers get away with this because it is not worth their time to be active participants in corporate monitoring—they are rationally ignorant and follow the Wall Street rule of selling their shares rather than complaining about poor performance.

The economic approach to the corporation builds on this tradition and refers to the "separation of ownership and control" as an agency problem—the managerial agents do not always have the incentives to act in the shareholders' best interests. Agency theory characterizes the corporation as a "nexus of contracts" among shareholders, managers, directors, creditors, and employees who voluntarily join together in mutually beneficial transactions.[2] In this economic model, agency costs are the sum, first, of the costs of managers pursuing their own interests at the expense of shareholder value and, second, of the costs of resources devoted to dealing with this problem. It is irrational and wastes shareholder value to attempt to align managerial interests perfectly with shareholder interests because the costs of perfect control exceed the benefits. In other words, the optimal amount of self-interested conduct by managers, both for shareholders and for society as a whole, is more than zero.

Agency theory provides a useful framework for thinking about the role of SOX in protecting shareholder value from managerial malfeasance. In the extreme, we can stop all such malfeasance only by outlawing the corporation and forcing businesspeople to stop hiring agents.

How do we determine the optimal amount of fraud? In other words, how much fraud should shareholders be expected to tolerate? One approach is to put it in the context of efficient markets and risk-bearing by shareholders. Efficient securities markets discount the known risk of fraud in the price of securities based on factors such as the nature of the industry and the track records of key executives. This forces firms to deal with these risks if they want to raise new capital. To be sure, some of the risk of fraud cannot be quantified. But shareholders are assumed to own a portfolio of stocks through which they diversify many different risks, including the risks of managerial ineptitude, managerial entrenchment, accounting and other fraud, self-dealing, and lawsuits. Thus, through diversification, shareholders can minimize their costs of bearing the risk of fraud. A corollary is that attempting to eliminate all managerial malfeasance would actually hurt diversified shareholders by requiring managers to devote resources to reducing risks that shareholders can deal with cheaply on their own.

Consistent with this market structure, our corporate governance system allows managers to take reasonable business risks on behalf of shareholders. These risks would include strategic decisions in entering markets, mergers and acquisitions, research and development, and organizational control issues—for instance, how much to invest in internal controls such as monitoring employee performance. All of these business decisions are protected from state law fiduciary liability by the business judgment rule, which allows managers to take reasonably informed risks without fear of second-guessing by litigious shareholders with 20/20 hindsight.[3]

SOX section 404, which is discussed in detail in chapter 4, is a good example of a misguided attempt to eliminate all agency costs. This section requires executives to certify the adequacy of their internal controls. The discussion below will demonstrate that the internal controls requirement does not reflect a tradeoff of costs and benefits that is in the best interests of shareholders. Shareholders are not interested in perfect internal controls for the sake of control. They are only interested in improving internal controls if the improvement will increase share value. Yet the early results from the section 404 internal controls attestations indicate that, although less than 8 percent of the largest 2,500 corporations found deficiencies, all firms were required to invest millions of dollars to identify these problems. This suggests that diversified investors would be better off without section 404. In the absence of SOX, corporate boards and executives would have been guided by rational cost-benefit analysis in determining the extent of controls and the appropriate amount of documentation.

3

Imagining a World without SOX

Defenders do not mince words in claiming that SOX is a tremendous success. For example, Harvey Goldschmidt, a former SEC commissioner and strong proponent of the reforms, states, "I think that Sarbanes-Oxley has been a great success in terms of the effect it has had on improved corporate governance. There is no question it has been a great piece of legislation, and anybody who says otherwise is talking like a darn fool."[1] And Representative Michael Oxley—not a "darn fool"—suggests that the issue of benefits transcends data:

> No one can know with any accuracy . . . where we would be today had Sarbanes-Oxley not been created. . . . How can you measure the value of knowing that company books are sounder than they were before? Of no more overnight bankruptcies with the employees and retirees left holding the bag? No more disruption to entire sectors of the economy? I think that's a valuable return for the investment, when the outlays now are a small fraction of the losses that were sustained.[2]

This sort of thinking obviously puts a strong burden of proof on opponents of regulation. Indeed, to the extent Oxley suggests that the value of the legislation cannot be measured, the burden is impossible to bear.

The burden should, instead, be on proponents of massive new regulation. The overwhelming success and strength of our capital markets, and the dominance of private contracting, suggest that the market works without new regulation, and that regulations should thus be required to pass a cost-benefit test. And, contrary to Oxley's assertion, there are ways to measure both costs and benefits, as demonstrated by the finance studies summarized below in chapter 4. Although these metrics are imperfect, they can, cumulatively, provide some guidance to regulators if carefully done and understood.

The analysis should begin with a realistic appraisal of the benefits that have flowed from SOX. It is important to understand that much of what SOX sought to accomplish might have been done at much lower cost by markets alone or under state law without the need for a broad and burdensome new federal regime.

To frame this analysis, assume for the moment that there is less fraud in the post-SOX world. This chapter asks if there would have been more fraud over the past three and a half years in the absence of the act. Some of the improvement may have nothing to do with SOX. But even if some market improvement can be traced to it, it is far from clear that it would not have been provided by the markets or the states, perhaps more efficiently, if SOX had not been adopted. If Congress had not acted, others might have, and there were already ample mechanisms in place to protect against further frauds. Issuers, securities firms, and other market actors had even stronger incentives than Congress to restore "confidence in the market" if, as Congress believed, lack of confidence were driving away their customers and sources of capital.[3]

This chapter shows that there are many things corporations, private organizations, and states might have done if Congress had not passed SOX. It also shows that these alternatives might have been at least as effective as SOX in reducing managerial malfeasance and fraud, and concludes that the act has interfered with the operation of these important corporate governance devices.

Capital Market Forces

Even without SOX or any other law, the capital market would continue monitoring corporations, backed by the extensive mandatory disclosure laws already on the books. Even in the absence of private or public regulation, markets had the capacity to address the problems that surfaced in Enron and related scandals. Here we discuss some of the available alternatives.

Market Monitoring. SOX was Congress's response to the particular frauds revealed in Enron, WorldCom, and other cases. For example, auditors and lawyers failed to spot or report fraud, so Congress passed provisions mandating reporting and greater independence of these gatekeepers. Bernie Ebbers and WorldCom demonstrated the problems that loans to insiders could cause when not carefully monitored, so Congress decided to ban them.

Securities analysts, investment managers, and others have a strong financial motive to ferret out information. How can the market spot fraud, which by definition is hidden? The same information about past frauds and disclosure lapses that Congress relied on in passing SOX now can inform market actors as to what to look for in the firms they watch. Analysts now know, for example, to look more closely at the fine print in financial statement footnotes and to rely more on "hard" numbers, such as free cash flow, rather than "soft" numbers affected by firms' decisions on capitalizing and amortizing expenses, unusually high rates of growth, and arrogant managers.[4]

Companies also provide information in the form of the mechanisms they adopt, or fail to adopt, to monitor for fraud. Financial economists are doing significant theoretical modeling and empirical research to determine which corporate practices and characteristics are correlated with financial risk. For example, researchers showed that the more nonaudit services corporations bought from their audit firms, the more they were likely to "manage" earnings. The market evidently caught on to this, because the same study showed that investors tended to devalue firms that disclosed unexpected purchases of nonaudit services.[5] There is also evidence that firms subject to SEC enforcement actions from 1978 to 2002 incurred total market penalties, as measured by expected loss in the present value of future cash flows due to higher contracting and financing costs, that were twelve times the total of SEC and private litigation penalties imposed on these firms.[6] These penalties were visited not only on firms, but also on their managers. Another study has shown increased management turnover following earnings restatements, and indicated that the employment prospects of the displaced managers of restatement firms are poorer than those of the displaced managers of firms that have not issued restatements.[7]

In the post-Enron environment, firms would similarly put investors on alert if they gave large loans to executives, had executives on the board audit committee, or used other governance mechanisms that the market has condemned. The firms could decide whether the benefits they obtain from these devices outweigh the increase in capital costs. They also would have incentives to adopt market-favored devices, and to signal in other ways that they are well-managed, as discussed later in this chapter.

To be sure, market monitoring may not work without mandatory disclosure. But a well-developed mandatory disclosure system already exists. The question for federal regulators and Congress should have been whether this system ought to have been tweaked to give the market the information it needs. This approach would have preserved the traditional distinction, entrenched for seventy years, between the federal emphasis on disclosure and the state emphasis on internal governance.

In fact, even before Enron's collapse and the advent of SOX, analysts had a lot of the information they needed to be able to spot fraud. For example, in February 2001, eight months before the disclosures that brought Enron down, a hedge fund manager figured out that Enron had been using derivatives to speculate rather than to hedge.[8] The footnotes to Enron's financial statements disclosed the basic facts concerning the company's potential exposure to debts incurred by special-purpose entities.[9]

If all these facts were available, why did it take so long for the market to catch on? The answer is that the market was in a boom cycle. "New-economy" firms were exploring methods of doing business for which evaluation metrics had not been developed. Analysts and executives were arguing that the established guidelines for price-earnings multiples did not apply to novel business methods. Optimistic day-traders, flush with cash, were inclined to agree.

So was SOX necessary to prevent future market vulnerability to fraud? The existence of a repetitive cycle of periods of boom, bust, and regulation strongly suggests not. As noted above, the market disregarded information that was actually in the disclosure documents of firms like Enron. To be sure, this was not clear disclosure—it had to be ferreted out by analysts. But once that had been done, the warning signs were in the open, inviting more careful investigation and evaluation. Perhaps curious analysts would have hit stone walls within the companies, but the absence of information (and a company's unwillingness to provide it) suggests the presence of risk which, in turn, is reflected in the market price.

Moreover, even if more disclosure, or perhaps the barring of suspect practices, would have prevented Enron and other frauds, it is not clear that such regulations will prevent the next fraud—which will not be about special-purpose entities or derivatives, but probably about some other practices that neither the markets nor Congress can now anticipate. With or without SOX, the possibility of another major Enron-like corporate fraud would inevitably persist.

Reputations and Signaling. The primary political argument for the passage of SOX was the political need to "restore investor confidence." Although there is good reason to doubt the economic validity of this argument, an underlying theoretical argument supports regulation if the post-fraud securities market is a market for "lemons" that investors will avoid because all investments, like the inventory on a shady used car lot, look like potential losers. This refers to the theory of George Akerlof, the 2001 Nobel laureate in economics.[10] It follows from this insight that regulation like SOX is not so much for the benefit of investors, who will avoid future risk, but for that of reputable sellers who will lose business unless they can persuade buyers that the sharks are gone and it is safe to swim.

The question is whether regulation is necessary to reassure investors. Akerlof shared his Nobel Prize with Michael Spence and Joseph Stiglitz for their work on market responses to the lemons problem.[11] In the present context, these would include firms' maintaining good reputations for honesty and signaling to investors and others that they are not like Enron or WorldCom.

Firms' reputations provide an important way to protect investors. Firms invest significant sums in advertising and in behavior that induces investors to trust them and thereby reduce their cost of capital.[12] Firms that cheat incur a significant penalty by devaluing the reputation they spent so much to build. This effect was observed recently in mutual funds that suffered significant outflow of funds after news reports of misbehavior.[13]

Signals include maintaining a high level of voluntary formal disclosure, voluntarily joining organizations or obtaining certifications from reputational intermediaries, having candid meetings with securities analysts and the media, or voluntarily adopting mechanisms suggested by governance reformers, such as expensing stock options, separating audit and nonaudit services, or hiring auditing firms that follow this practice.

Firms also can signal by buying insurance, since the size of the premium indicates the extent of the insured risk. This is a fairly reliable signal, since insurance firms have strong incentives to set the price accurately, and firms' incentives to insure minimize the risk of false signals. There is evidence that the liability insurance premiums of firms' directors and officers accurately indicate the quality of their governance arrangements.[14] Firms also might signal honesty by buying "financial statement insurance," in which the insurance carrier hires the auditor and provides the signal.[15]

An advantage of signaling over mandatory regulation is that each firm can decide whether the benefits of signaling integrity outweigh the costs. For example, some firms may derive substantial benefits from having their auditors do nonaudit services, and they may have in place alternative monitoring systems that reduce the need for this extra assurance of disinterested auditing. One-size-fits-all regulation precludes this sort of tailoring.

Moreover, mandatory regulation may carry the extra cost of discouraging or disabling potentially valuable signaling. Once the law requires all firms to adhere to the same standard, they have less incentive to signal their integrity. This reduces market incentives to develop and adopt alternative signaling mechanisms. For example, in the absence of SOX, a market in financial statement insurance might have developed that would permit more precise and cost-effective measurement of fraud risk.

Given the potential for signaling to restore confidence in the market on a firm-by-firm basis, the main theoretical defense of SOX is as a subsidy for firms that have relatively high costs of using these mechanisms. One might argue that, without SOX, newer and smaller issuers, which are riskier because the market has less information about them, might have struggled in a risk-sensitive post-Enron market as compared to their bigger and more reputable rivals. But this would be an ironic defense of SOX, given the outcry concerning the problems the act—particularly its internal controls provisions—creates for smaller firms (see chapter 4). If SOX-type regulation is, indeed, better for smaller firms, then it should be designed with the needs and characteristics of these firms in mind. Clearly, SOX did not meet this alleged need.

Shareholder Monitoring

Even if SOX had never become law, firms would be subject to scrutiny not only by the capital markets, but also by their own shareholders. Highly visible institutional shareholders like TIAA-CREF have the clout to press for changes by directly communicating with managers and by enlisting support from other shareholders through shareholder proposals that the firm must subsidize under current SEC rules.[16] Managers would risk market penalties by not responding favorably to proposals that receive significant support. The proposals also could provide information to the SEC as to the extent to which shareholders—whose money is on the line—favor particular reform initiatives.

To be sure, institutional investors such as state pension funds may have their own political agendas, and individual investors lack incentives to spearhead governance reform. But there are also very motivated investors who can institute reform by buying large or controlling interests. The active takeover market of the 1980s was killed by the combination of federal prosecutions of the key players, the Williams Act, and state anti-takeover laws. Indeed, the weakened market for corporate control that resulted from this regulation may partly account for the recent corporate frauds. However, a new market for control has been revived through hedge and private equity funds. These buyers have much more high-powered monitoring incentives than the independent directors, auditors, and lawyers on whom SOX relies so heavily.

The more general lesson from the recent history of takeovers concerns the efficacy of regulation. Takeover regulation was supposed to be the solution to the last problem of excessive job insecurity for managers and workers. It did little to address this problem, while helping to weaken governance and thereby create conditions for the next crisis of corporate fraud. The lesson is that additional market regulation may have unforeseeable perverse effects and should be approached with caution rather than embraced in panic.

State and International Competition

Even without SOX, there would still have been the substantial body of state corporate law, which historically, and even after SOX, has been the principal mechanism for regulating corporate governance. SOX, however, represented a significant shift away from state law in its provisions prescribing the composition of board audit committees, prohibiting certain officer loans, and requiring reimbursement of bonuses and stock profits. Even SOX's disclosure provisions, particularly including the internal controls disclosures, may have indirectly invaded state regulation of corporate governance by establishing a de facto governance standard.

The state-based system of regulating corporate governance has been hailed as one of the main strengths of the U.S. capital markets.[17] Although William Cary, a former SEC chairman, famously decried the competition for corporate charters as a "race to the bottom," Ralph Winter quickly pointed out that Cary had ignored the fact that efficient capital markets ensure that firms' incorporation decisions are capitalized into the value of their shares.[18] There is significant evidence based on stock returns indicating that firms' incorporation decisions are, in fact, efficient.[19]

There are also strong advantages inherent to adjudication of corporate issues in state courts. As two prominent Delaware judges remarked recently:

> In our experience, the effective adjudication of corporate law disputes requires a great deal of direct involvement by the trial judge. The factual records in such cases are often large and make for demanding reading. Moreover, many of these matters are time-sensitive and involve the application of complex legal doctrines to the evidence in a very short timeframe—a reality that limits the capacity of judges to delegate very much of the work to law clerks. As we understand it, the federal courts already face a stiff challenge in addressing their already formidable caseloads. . . . In view of that reality, it seems unlikely that the federal courts are well-positioned to absorb the burden of adjudicating corporate governance disputes now handled by state courts.[20]

Some might argue that Enron and other frauds indicated a failure of state corporate law. But it is interesting that two of the main culprits, Enron and WorldCom, were not incorporated in the leading jurisdiction of Delaware, but rather in Oregon and Georgia, respectively. These firms' choice of state law may have been based on an expectation of favorable regulatory treatment or better protection against takeovers than in Delaware.[21] In the wake of Enron, firms might have been more careful in eschewing these considerations and focusing on whether the chosen regime protects shareholders against managerial agency costs. This would also encourage Delaware to respond to the heightened concern with agent misconduct.[22]

Moreover, before blaming state law and turning to more federal law, we should consider that a regulatory landscape already increasingly dominated by federal law was ineffective in preventing Enron.

It is not obvious that even more federal law is the answer. Mark Roe has argued persuasively that the ever-present threat of federalization necessarily constrains states in regulating corporate governance.[23] As discussed below, SOX may have tightened this noose and further disabled the states from responding to corporate governance problems.

Relying on state law would better enable firms to tailor their governance to their particular circumstances. For example, the evidence indicates that more board independence is not correlated with firm value.[24] A review of state laws on executive loans, which were supplanted by SOX's prohibition of many such loans, indicates significant variation, from prescribing procedures for approval to requiring the board to identify a corporate benefit, or providing for no default regulation at all.[25]

Theoretically, the advantages of state competition might be extended to the international scene, with international jurisdictional competition as to disclosure rules.[26] Foreign firms already can choose to "bond" their integrity by cross-listing in the United States or other jurisdictions, thereby subjecting themselves to these legal regimes in addition to those in their home countries. Substantial evidence supports this bonding explanation of cross-listing.[27] Full-fledged international competition currently is hobbled by the fact that the United States insists on regulating all trading within its borders regardless of where the firms are based. Thus, if international competition is not as successful as state competition, it is because of the overreaching of federal law. Piling on more federal law through SOX aggravates rather than reduces this problem.

Regulation by Stock Exchanges and Other Private Institutions

Finally, it is worth wondering whether private organizations might have picked up any regulatory slack that existed in the absence of SOX. Firms can supplement market discipline by subjecting themselves to regulation by nongovernmental bodies. In a manner similar to the signaling discussed above, a firm's decision to be regulated would be evaluated by the capital markets and reflected in its stock price.

Firms already are subject to governance provisions in stock exchange listing agreements. Exchanges theoretically have an incentive to compete for listings by offering rules that reduce listed firms' cost of capital.[28] Thus, shortly after SOX was passed, the New York Stock Exchange Board of Directors adopted listing standards relating to director independence that went beyond the act's regulation of audit committee membership.[29] The NYSE, for example, has an incentive in competing with NASDAQ and other exchanges to encourage firms to pay higher listing fees in exchange for a lower cost of capital by assuring investors in those firms that the NYSE is actively monitoring them.[30]

Other types of self-regulatory organizations might also play a significant role in monitoring firms. There is evidence, for example, that peer review and competition among professional auditing associations can provide effective monitoring of auditing firms.[31]

The upshot of the analysis and evidence presented in this chapter is that the American corporate governance system has numerous self-correcting forces that are likely to be more focused and more measured than an economy-wide regulatory intervention such as SOX. Neither Congress nor SOX's defenders give credit to the historical, institutional strengths of our corporate governance system. A greater appreciation of the market forces and institutional incentives leads to the inevitable conclusion that there was little opportunity for Congress to add much value. In short, the benefits of SOX necessarily have been slight. Unfortunately, as detailed below, SOX's costs have been enormous.

4

The Costs of SOX

Many defenders focus on these direct compliance costs and reassure us that they are temporary, will decline as firms figure out how to comply, and, in any event, are worth it if the result is reducing fraud. Their assessments, however, are based on an overly sanguine view of what SOX compliance actually entails, and a failure to realize what a heavy weight it ties around the legs of U.S. firms. Among other things, SOX has diverted attention from the hard work of maximizing shareholder value and distorted executives' incentives and investment decisions. As discussed in chapter 6, the most extensive and persuasive study of SOX's financial costs estimates the loss in total market value of firms around legislative events leading to its passage at $1.4 trillion.[1] This astronomical amount suggests that the stock markets implicitly estimated the net costs of SOX to be much greater than simply the present value of the future direct costs of compliance. The lesson from chapter 2 was that the risk of corporate fraud and agent misconduct does not necessarily justify regulation if the costs of the regulation exceed the costs of the fraud and misconduct that would occur in the absence of regulation. Although SOX was ostensibly passed to protect investors, it hurts them if it forces corporations to spend more on protection than they are gaining in fraud reduction. It is useful to recall the 1976 swine flu scare, in which one person died from the disease and thirty-two from the vaccine.

This chapter considers some sources of SOX's direct and indirect costs.

Direct Compliance Costs

First we discuss the direct compliance costs imposed by SOX that have attracted the most media attention.

Section 404 Internal Controls Disclosures and Attestation. Consistent with the philosophy of the original 1933 and 1934 federal securities acts, SOX increases mandated disclosure in several areas. Perhaps the most troublesome new provision has been section 404, which imposes a brand-new and extensive obligation on managers to assess the quality of their internal controls. Little discussed or debated in Congress, and little noticed during the whirlwind of July 2002, it provides for SEC rules requiring that firms' annual reports

> contain an internal control report, which shall—(1) state the responsibility of management for establishing and maintaining an adequate internal control structure and procedures for financial reporting; and (2) contain an assessment, as of the end of the most recent fiscal year of the issuer, of the effectiveness of the internal control structure and procedures of the issuer for financial reporting.

Section 404 acquires extra importance because of two other sections of the law requiring senior executives to take personal responsibility for these new annual report disclosures. Section 302 provides for SEC rules requiring senior officers to certify in each annual or quarterly report not only that they know of no material misstatements or omissions in the report, but that they

> (A) are responsible for establishing and maintaining internal controls; (B) have designed such internal controls to ensure that material information relating to the issuer and its consolidated subsidiaries is made known to such officers by others within those entities, particularly

during the period in which the periodic reports are being prepared; (C) have evaluated the effectiveness of the issuer's internal controls as of a date within 90 days prior to the report; and (D) have presented in the report their conclusions about the effectiveness of their internal controls based on their evaluation as of that date.

The officers must certify that they have disclosed to the firm's auditors and board audit committee

significant deficiencies in the design or operation of internal controls which could adversely affect the issuer's ability to record, process, summarize, and report financial data and have identified for the issuer's auditors any material weaknesses in internal controls; and . . . any fraud, whether or not material, that involves management or other employees who have a significant role in the issuer's internal controls.

Finally, the signing officers must indicate "significant changes in internal controls or in other factors that could significantly affect internal controls" since the last evaluation.

Section 906 requires the issuer's CEO and CFO to certify that

the periodic report containing the financial statements fully complies with the requirements of section 13(a) or 15(d) of the Securities Exchange Act of 1934 (15 U.S.C. 78m or 78o(d)) and that information contained in the periodic report fairly presents, in all material respects, the financial condition and results of operations of the issuer.

These requirements include, of course, the internal controls disclosures under section 404.

The SEC has, in fact, issued voluminous rules implementing and interpreting these provisions.[2] To give a taste of the rules, they clarify that the officers must sign off on, among other things, whether trans-actions are recorded as necessary, and provide assurances regarding unauthorized acquisition, use, or sale of assets.[3] Changes potentially affecting internal controls that the officers must evaluate include significant corporate transactions, expansion into new regions, and changes in management or organizational structure.[4] The SEC has also made clear that management must follow methodologies that recognized bodies have established after public comment.[5]

SOX also requires external auditors to opine on both managers' assessments and their own evaluations of control effectiveness.[6] The provision was implemented by Auditing Standard No. 2, promul-gated by the Public Company Accounting Oversight Board (PCAOB), the auditor regulator that SOX created (and whose appointment is the basis of the Free Enterprise Fund lawsuit mentioned in chapter 1). Sec-tion 404 created a new standard of what potential problems needed to be disclosed—specifically, "significance" rather than the traditional test of "materiality." This standard will have to be developed through many years of case law and SEC rulemaking. In the meantime, firms and auditors have to guess how the test will be applied.

The SEC initially estimated that its proposed rules implementing SOX section 404 "would impose an additional 5 burden hours per issuer in connection with each quarterly and annual report."[7] This estimate was sharply rebuked in comments on the proposed rule.[8] The SEC's final rule revised the estimate up to "around . . . $91,000 per company," not including "additional cost burdens that a com-pany will incur as a result of having to obtain an auditor's attesta-tion."[9] Moreover, the SEC was way off the mark even after it revised its cost estimates. For example, Financial Executives International estimated compliance costs at $4.36 million per company as of mid-2005, and AMR Research has estimated that companies will spend $6 billion to comply with SOX in 2006.[10] One can only wonder how the SEC (or plaintiffs' attorneys) would react to errors and restatements of similar magnitude by a publicly traded corporation.

There was an outcry from firms as the internal controls rule kicked in for financial statements due after November 15, 2004— an outcry so intense that it may have accounted in part for the early departure of SEC chairman William Donaldson. The SEC responded in several ways to the concerns about internal controls reporting—by delaying reporting by small and foreign companies; by convening an advisory committee on smaller public companies, which has recommended exemptions of, or at least modified requirements for, smaller companies; and by a roundtable in April 2005.[11] These were followed by a May 16 policy statement and joined by a policy statement from the PCAOB on implementing the internal controls audits. The policy statement observed:

> Although it is not surprising that first-year implementa-tion of Section 404 was challenging, almost all of the significant complaints we heard related not to the Sarbanes-Oxley Act or to the rules and auditing standards implementing Section 404, but rather to a mechanical, and even overly cautious, way in which those rules and standards apparently have been applied in many cases. Both management and external auditors must bring rea-soned judgment and a top-down, risk-based approach to the 404 compliance process. A one-size fits all, bottom-up, check-the-box approach that treats all controls equally is less likely to improve internal controls and financial reporting than reasoned, good faith exercise of professional judgment focused on reasonable, as opposed to absolute, assurance.[12]

The upshot of these initiatives, as described in a speech last November by SEC commissioner Cynthia Glassman, is that Glass-man was "still hearing stories of auditors identifying over 40,000 key controls and, while significant reductions in auditors' fees were pro-jected at the time of the roundtable, recent anecdotal reports suggest that such fee reductions have not yet materialized."[13]

It should not be surprising that the SEC's and PCAOB's jawbon-ing were not enough to "bring reasoned judgment and a risk-based approach" to the process.[14] As will be discussed further, the prob-lem is that auditors, corporate executives who also sign off on financial statements, and corporations must fear not only regulatory sanctions if they understate risks and the need for controls, but also civil litigation and criminal prosecutions the next time inherent business uncertainty drives a firm's price down.

One striking thing about the controversy over the costs of compliance with section 404 is that, even though they are much higher than anyone in the government predicted, no one in Congress or the SEC is advocating reconsidering the propriety of section 404—although there is some concern about its adverse impact on smaller firms. SOX's defenders dismiss the problem as one of startup costs that will be amortized over time. But many of the costs are ongoing and are likely to remain high, even if lower than during the initial period.[15]

Another striking thing about the controversy is that it was so predictable. Precisely the same thing happened when Congress adopted the first major set of internal controls in 1977 in the Foreign Corrupt Practices Act. The controversy was quelled only when the SEC adopted an interpretation and policy statement.[16] If Congress had done its homework, it would have foreseen the problems that would result from SOX's much broader internal controls provision.

Audit Committee Independence. Corporate reformers long have loved the idea that directors who are not employed full-time by the company and who are otherwise independent of the company and its insiders will aggressively monitor executives' performance on behalf of shareholders. They have ignored theoretical questions, such as why it is logical to assume that one who is employed full-time elsewhere would have adequate time, incentives, and information to be effective, or why any problems with nonindependent directors would not be reflected in share price. They have also ignored the ample data showing that corporate profitability is generally unrelated to the number of independent directors on the board.[17]

The specific SOX contribution to board structure was to ensure that a company's auditors are chosen and overseen by a fully independent audit committee. This focus was not surprising, given the lapses in oversight by Enron's auditor, Arthur Andersen. But as

Congress rushed to act in the headlong process discussed in chapter 1, nobody asked the right questions about whether any of this could have been prevented by requiring more independence. Remarkably, nobody seems to have cared that the Enron audit committee was independent. Nobody inquired as to the difficulty directors faced in overseeing auditors. Nobody wondered whether this fix was necessary or effective in addition to SOX's provisions applying directly to audit firms. Nobody asked, is it worth the cost for firms to pay both the increased audit costs under the act and the increased costs of audit committees? Nor did anyone ask whether any but the largest companies could afford the stringent new audit committee requirements, or what these requirements would mean to foreign issuers subject to SOX with board structures very different from those of U.S. companies.

The data before and after SOX lend little support to the notion that the benefits of increased audit committee independence are worth the costs. Roberta Romano reviews sixteen studies attempting to relate audit committee independence to various performance measures and finds that ten fail to show that audit committee independence improves performance, one reports inconsistent results for different models, and three of the remaining studies suffer from methodological flaws.[18] The factor that seems to matter more in the studies than independence is whether the audit committee members are financially sophisticated.

Rules requiring independent directors may be much more burdensome for small than for large firms. One study found that small firms paid $5.91 to nonemployee directors per $1,000 in sales before SOX, compared with $9.76 per $1,000 in sales after SOX, while large firms' costs increased only from $.13 to $.15 per $1,000 in sales.[19] This disproportionate impact on small firms stifles entrepreneurial incentives and, in effect, denies access to public capital markets.

Managing in the Shadow of SOX

SOX is a burdensome intrusion into the internal affairs of public companies. This could be justified by regulators if it corrected a market failure and resulted in benefits greater than costs. However, as discussed above, the benefits are likely small, and the costs are very high.

Section 404 Internal Controls. As we have seen, section 404 of SOX, its so-called "internal controls" provision, involves serious direct compliance costs. SOX defenders argue that these costs are worth the deterrence to fraud that internal controls reporting and certification provide. But it is harder to justify the significant long-term effects such reporting has on business.[20]

First, modern firms, unlike the small shops of the early nineteenth century, rely on specialization of functions, automation, delegation of authority, and complex hierarchies. Managers have to be able to trust their subordinates. SOX raises a serious question whether this sort of trust is consistent with the need to have adequate "controls." SOX will surely provoke redundancies that detract from bureaucratic efficiency.

Second, SOX clearly penalizes change and innovation. Any upgrades, new software, or acquisitions would have to be evaluated as "significant changes in internal controls or in other factors that could significantly affect internal controls." The safer course, when in doubt, is to do nothing.

Third, SOX requires firms to devote significant resources not only to tracking information, but to providing a costly and unnecessary paper trail. For example, the SEC's rule defining executives' certification obligations says that

> an assessment of the effectiveness of internal control over financial reporting must be supported by evidential matter, including documentation, regarding both the design of internal controls and the testing processes. This evidential matter should provide reasonable support: for the evaluation of whether the control is designed to prevent or detect material misstatements or omissions; for the conclusion that the tests were appropriately planned and performed; and that the results of the tests were appropriately considered.[21]

Of course, firms need to find and discipline fraud. But, as we have repeatedly emphasized, they will be less profitable if they have to spend more on preventing fraud than the fraud was costing them.

The risks imposed by the internal controls provision fall directly on auditors or executives who sign off on the internal controls reports. Since auditors and executives are less able to bear risk than the shareholders of publicly held firms who hold diversified portfolios, the auditors and executives may respond by either demanding greater compensation or adjusting their behavior to reduce the risk. Indeed, one study finds a post-SOX decline in the ratio of incentive compensation to salary after the passage of SOX, and in firms' research and development expenses and capital expenditures.[22] These results indirectly indicate reduced manager incentives to invest in, and be compensated based upon, the riskier long term. Ultimately, the shareholders bear most of this risk.

Impact on Managerial Risk-Taking: Independent Directors. SOX requires audit committees to be made up entirely of independent directors. This seemed like a reasonable response to the accounting scandals because it appeared that senior executives had been able to dominate the auditors and audit committees of Enron, WorldCom, and others. As mentioned above, board independence has long been a favorite panacea of corporate governance reformers, despite questions about its cost-effectiveness. Those questions aside, Peter Wallison has offered an argument that independence can actually be harmful:

> The independent directors of a company are part-timers. No matter how astute in the ways of business and finance, they know much less about the business of the companies they are charged with overseeing than the CEOs and other professional managers who run these enterprises day to day. Unfamiliarity in turn breeds caution and conservatism. When asked to choose between a risky course that could result in substantial

increases in company profits or a more cautious approach that has a greater chance to produce the steady gains of the past, independent directors are very likely to choose the safe and sure. They have little incentive to take risk and multiple reasons to avoid it.[23]

Constraining Executive Compensation: Insider Loan Prohibitions. Executive compensation is a perennial hot button issue in corporate governance, yet SOX did not directly address the area. Perhaps Congress was mindful of the perverse incentives created by its last foray into executive compensation, in 1993, when it limited the tax deductibility of executive pay to $1 million annually unless it was "performance-based."[24] This law naturally encouraged more reliance on stock options which, in turn, increased managers' incentives to manage earnings and focus on short-term results.[25] Moreover, a predictable result of this reform is that executives increasingly will be rewarded based on "random" components of company performance rather than the results of their own efforts.[26] Now concern about excessive managerial compensation has spurred a massive SEC effort to overhaul executive compensation disclosure.[27] This is likely to be only the beginning of more executive compensation "reform," as the cycle of misguided tinkering continues.

SOX's contribution to the executive compensation reform party was section 402, prohibiting insider loans. The problem with this regulation is that such loans have the potential benefit of encouraging insider ownership of company stock, which tends to align executives' interests with those of the shareholders.[28] To be sure, insider loans may have costs.[29] But Jayne Barnard suggests that Congress might have better balanced costs against benefits by examining the terms, purpose, and size of the loan, the company's expectations for repayment, the manner of approval, and the existence and extent of disclosure to investors. In other words, there is a vast difference between the mammoth questionable loans from WorldCom to CEO Bernie Ebbers and many of the other insider loans that SOX outlawed. Even if some regulation were efficient, it would have been better left to the states, which have a variety of strategies for dealing with these loans. Moreover, federal regulation might have taken several less intrusive forms, including enforcing existing disclosure laws, increasing disclosure, mandating particular approval or collection procedures, and prohibiting certain types of loans.[30]

Instead of this careful balancing of costs and benefits, Congress precipitously responded to the Republicans' need to reduce the damage from disclosures concerning the president's loans many years before, and to pressure from Senator Schumer's populist opportunism.[31]

Congress's action left many questions unanswered concerning the relationship between the loan prohibition and corporate practices currently authorized by state law, including advancement of attorneys' fees and expenses in litigation, agreements facilitating executives' exercise of stock options, and corporate payment of life insurance premiums for executives.[32] Even Sarbanes and Oxley expressed disagreement about whether clarification was necessary.[33] In desperation, after receiving little official clarification, lawyers from twenty-five large law firms drafted their own guidance, only to leave themselves open to a charge that they had violated the antitrust laws.[34] The SEC's Advisory Committee on Smaller Public Companies has recommended that the SEC clarify various aspects of this provision, noting that it has not yet done so.[35] Such confusion and waste of legal talent are additional indirect costs of SOX.

Lawyer Monitoring. SOX section 307 calls for the SEC to promulgate a rule "requiring an attorney to report evidence of a material violation of securities law or breach of fiduciary duty or similar violation by the company or any agent thereof" to the chief legal counsel or chief executive officer, and, if they do not respond, to the audit committee, other independent directors, or the board. This provision was a response to well-publicized reports that Enron's outside lawyers had failed adequately to act on information they had concerning misdeeds within the company.

After SOX, the SEC had to figure out how lawyers could fulfill their reporting obligation. An important part of the SEC's rule was to permit corporations to set up something called a Qualified Legal Compliance Committee (QLCC) as a reporting mechanism. Two commentators criticized this innovation as "likely to increase the cost to issuers of obtaining and retaining high-quality directors, increase the demands on scarce director time, and . . . interfere with board collegiality and board-management relations."[36]

An empirical study of how the QLCC rule has actually functioned showed that, while the SEC had predicted 3,620 issuers would form QLCCs, the number by mid-September 2005 was only 556, about 3 percent of eligible firms.[37] The main problem, the author found, was that lawyers and directors believed this structure inappropriately shifted responsibility for legal compliance decisions away from the managers, where it had traditionally been, and onto the board, which is not equipped to determine how to handle legal risk. This, of course, means that the board may have to bear legal liability for not acting on risks that are identified by reports to their QLCCs. On the other hand, investment funds and trusts have been more willing to form QLCCs, since those firms do not have separate managerial employees, and they welcome this opportunity for dealing with potential conflicts of interest by their investment advisors. This study sheds light on the main problem with SOX section 307 and, indirectly, on a central problem with SOX: Even if some adjustment in relationships between corporations and their lawyers is justified, by regulating the details of the relationships, SOX risks interfering with structures that are firmly entrenched under state law and current practice, with unpredictable and potentially costly results.

Another potential problem with section 307 is that removing relationships with lawyers from operating management and putting them into the hands of independent directors erects a barrier between firms' managers and the professional advisors these managers must deal with every day.[38] If changes in lawyer monitoring are necessary, there are ways to make them cost-effectively through the structure of professional firms and ethical rules. Clearly, lawyer monitoring not only is a waste of legal talent but also unnecessarily disrupts candid communications and traditional hierarchical relationships.

Monitoring by Corporate Executives. SOX increases monitoring duties of corporate executives by requiring them to certify reports and internal controls. This forces them to immerse themselves in the minutiae of their firms which, as will be discussed, may not be an efficient use of valuable managerial resources. Also, imposing litigation risk on individual managers is likely to make them insist on precautions and paperwork that diversified shareholders would find excessively costly. Thus, the executive certification requirements add to the costs of the internal controls requirements. Moreover, as discussed below in chapter 5, the litigation risk inherent in the certification requirements may contribute to excessive timidity in corporate management. With potentially billions of dollars in liability at stake, the most profitable corporations subject to SOX will be the ones whose executives are well-trained to anticipate litigation difficulties rather than deal with business issues.

Building the Paper Trail. SOX imposes complex new record-keeping obligations on corporations. On the one hand, they have to document everything they do, creating a paper trail of explanations. On the other hand, if there is a fraud and an investigation, some email or other document that was innocuous at the time it was created might be crucial evidence for the plaintiff if, in hindsight, it indicates a problem that should have been pursued. SOX will necessitate the development of a new field of expertise in corporate paper-shuffling. As will be discussed later in this chapter, the need for such expertise will divert managerial resources from more productive skills and tasks.

Whistleblowing. SOX section 806 subjects corporate executives to heightened scrutiny by protecting whistleblowing employees from reprisals. It was created in response to reports of attempts to squelch employee reports of the fraud at WorldCom, and to address the likelihood that many employees eventually will learn about aspects of any massive fraud.

Congress did not, however, sufficiently consider the potential costs of this provision. Most importantly, section 806 essentially creates a new subtopic in employment law that hinders employers from efficiently monitoring their employees. Workers who "cause information to be provided" concerning a securities violation to the SEC, Congress, or "a person with supervisory authority over the employee," now have job protection under SOX. Given the open-ended language of the provision, an employee can threaten the firm with embarrassment even if his information is less than damning. Firms are likely to be litigating over, for example, when an employee "reasonably believes" that information shows a securities law violation and whether the job action was due to the whistleblowing.

Congress also obviously did not think long and hard over who should administer this new employment law. As it happens, it delegated enforcement to safety and health regulators, who have enough problems handling their main jobs without getting into the brave new world of financial fraud.[39]

Opportunity Costs of SOX

We have catalogued the various problems managers face in the wake of SOX, but we have not yet considered how much all this is going to cost. SOX's drafters and defenders seem to think that managers have plenty of time and energy, and that, as long as they do not have much else to do, they may as well spend time on the tasks SOX assigns to them. In fact, management energy and resources are scarce. What is spent on SOX compliance is not spent on other activities that may be more valuable to the firm and to society. This recalls Milton Friedman's admonition memorialized as "TANSTAAFL"—"There ain't no such thing as a free lunch."[40]

Diversion of Managerial Talent. SOX has demanded the attention of all board members and senior officers of every publicly traded company in America. It is very difficult to measure the opportunity cost of the time devoted to complying with SOX. For example, if a CEO whose annual salary is $1 million estimates that one-quarter of his time is devoted to complying with SOX, an accountant might calculate that the requirements cost the company

$250,000 in the CEO's time. However, the costs are surely much higher. The CEO is paid to add value—much more value than his salary.[41] The SOX mandates mean that the most talented American businesspeople must devote less time to increasing shareholder value than they otherwise would have been able to do, draining precious managerial resources at a time when U.S. businesses are subject to increasing competition from countries that are not saddled with SOX.

SOX not only diverts executive time from important managerial matters, but may be instrumental in diverting the executives themselves. Many executives are leaving public corporations, with their greatly increased risk of SOX liability, for the greener pastures of private equity.[42] The allocation of executive talent should depend on market opportunities, not federal regulation.

From Entrepreneurs to Hall Monitors. SOX is a problem not just for the firms that must incur high costs to comply, but because of the social costs from the business that does not get done and the firms that are not formed. SOX, in effect, represents a political judgment that less risk of fraud or bad business outcomes is necessarily good for society. Some social costs are attributable to the disproportionately high costs SOX imposes on smaller companies, discussed in the next section. The problem can arise, however, because of burdens imposed on larger firms as well.

First, the disproportionate compliance costs per dollar of capitalization for smaller firms impose social costs by discouraging startup ventures. The venture capital market is built on the assumption that successful startups financed by venture capital ultimately will exit from the venture phase into the public securities markets. To the extent that SOX is a tax on smaller public firms, it is therefore also a tax on entrepreneurial ventures.

Second, SOX imposes social costs by causing firms that have already been formed either to go private or to stay privately held. In this situation the owners, at least as a group, take the course of action that maximizes their wealth, given legal costs. However, there may be a social cost to the extent that public ownership of a firm offers gains to society as well as to the firm's owners. For one thing, public ownership enables diversification of risk, and thereby encourages entrepreneurial activity. Firms need to balance the higher agency costs of separating ownership and control against the advantages of risk diversification. A problem with SOX in this respect is that it forces at least some firms to accept a tax on public ownership for which they would not contract as a way of reducing agency costs. Society also may gain from public or community ownership of certain types of firms. For example, many firms going private in 2004 were community financial institutions, a type of firm for which public ownership may confer a social benefit.[43]

Third, SOX may reduce the flow of resources to riskier firms. Firms whose earnings are relatively variable, that engage in novel or more complex types of business for which the accounting standards are more uncertain, or that use novel business practices such as hedging and derivatives, are all subject to increased liability risk under SOX, particularly because of the greater need for disclosures about internal controls. This is supported by evidence that certain types of firms tend to find internal control problems—younger, smaller firms, and larger firms that are relatively complex and undergoing rapid change.[44] These additional risks may make it harder for them to find high-quality executives, auditors, and outside directors. Top executives may be attracted by more stable firms with lower liability risk, firms in less risky industries, or nonpublic companies not subject to SOX. They also might find jobs with better risk-reward profiles in consulting or auditing, given the need for these services under SOX. In other words, SOX may have the effect of shifting business from innovation and invention to simply looking for fraud.

Fourth, SOX may exact social costs by deterring acquisitions of smaller firms by larger ones. The SOX internal controls disclosure and certification requirements impose substantial burdens on firms acquiring new lines of business. These acquisitions, like going public, may be an important mechanism for financing entrepreneurial activity. They also may have the effect of moving assets to firms that are better able to minimize regulatory risks, or they may help reduce this risk by giving buyers an incentive to investigate risk and sellers an incentive to reduce it.[45] To be sure, SOX may also increase acquisitions because it increases the advantages firms derive from being big. But this happy circumstance of achieving economies of scale in SOX compliance would likely only occur with the merger of firms that had similar internal controls systems prior to the acquisition. Otherwise, the acquiring firm would have to invest considerable resources in harmonizing the control systems. Moreover, the economics of scale in compliance does not subtract from the costs of deterring acquisitions. Rather, it adds to social costs by encouraging acquisitions that would not be efficient without SOX.

Reducing Smaller Firms' Access to Public Capital Markets.
The internal controls rule also places a particularly heavy burden on smaller firms with significantly less benefit to investors. Evidence indicates that smaller and less actively traded firms react more unfavorably to events that increased the likelihood of SOX's passage.[46] In particular, smaller firms have higher overhead costs than larger ones, and therefore must struggle to compete with them. Any increase in overhead imposes an extra burden. Smaller firms compete, in part, through flexibility—the ability to change business plans rapidly to meet customer needs, and to combine functions in single individuals.

SOX delivers a dual hit to these firms by both imposing rigid and inflexible rules and increasing overhead costs. Moreover, these are not merely startup costs of compliance, but ongoing. Thus, it is not surprising to see that internal-controls reporting costs small firms more per dollar of capitalization or revenues than larger firms.[47] This effect is compounded for small firms in the startup phase, for which the risk assessment required by section 404 is likely to be more difficult. This may, in turn, reduce socially beneficial entrepreneurial activity.

Conversely, SOX's provisions, particularly its internal controls reporting, are inherently less beneficial for small than for large companies. The risks posed by small business failure to the economy are lower, since they represent only a small fraction of total market capitalization. Internal controls structures are less useful in small firms, which rely on top managers for control, and where these managers can, in any event, override internal controls. Given the lower benefits, it is not surprising that smaller firms have been more likely than larger ones to find weaknesses in internal controls when they set up these systems.[48]

The heavy burden SOX imposes on small firms has had the significant side effect of causing these firms to reduce their public ownership to avoid SOX. They can do this by becoming privately held or by "going dark"—that is, reducing the number of nominal public shareholders to below three hundred, which is the threshold for application of the Securities and Exchange Act of 1934, of which SOX is a part.[49]

SOX has clearly caused some firms to go private. This is indicated indirectly by evidence of post-SOX declines in small firms' share prices, and of share-price reactions to going private becoming more positive after enactment of SOX.[50] More directly, a recent paper compares the post-SOX rate of going private among American firms with the rate among foreign firms not subject to the act, thus controlling for non-SOX factors that could have caused firms to go private. It produces evidence consistent with the hypothesis that SOX induced small firms to become private during the first year following enactment.[51]

Why should we care if firms are going private?[52] The liquidity, risk-bearing, and informational advantages of public ownership potentially make them more valuable than they would be if they were closely held. To be sure, this does not mean that all firms should be public, but it does suggest it may be socially costly to, in effect, put a tax on public ownership. The whole point of SOX is supposedly to encourage public ownership by building "investor confidence." Unfortunately, the firms most in need of this "confidence," and therefore the ones SOX is purportedly helping the most, are the smaller, less-established firms that are, in fact, most disadvantaged by it.

Studies also have shown that 200 firms went dark in 2003, the year after SOX was enacted, that more firms went private after SOX, and that 44 of 114 firms that went private in 2004 cited SOX compliance costs as a reason. There is evidence that firms with higher audit fees were more likely to go dark, further linking going private with the costs of complying with SOX.[53]

Going dark means that firms stay public, since the three-hundred-shareholder minimum for registration includes shares held in "street name" on behalf of multiple beneficial holders. These firms lose disclosure transparency, which may help insiders but hurt outside shareholders who remain in the firm. Two studies show that firms lose share value when they announce they are going dark, and that, especially after SOX, going-dark transactions are positively correlated with insider ownership.[54] Firms might lose value from going dark because this transaction signals that they have fewer opportunities for growth, and therefore less need to make disclosures that would aid in raising capital. Indeed, the studies show that these firms do tend to have weaker growth potential.

But there is also evidence that firms that go dark have characteristics such as lower accounting quality and more free cash, indicating greater likelihood of insider misconduct.[55] In other words, they may have perverse reasons for wanting to avoid disclosure. Even before SOX, insiders could try to avoid disclosure obligations by going private and dark. But SOX's higher disclosure costs now give them a legitimate explanation. Even if this is the real explanation, SOX would be indirectly causing a loss of securities law protection for precisely those shareholders who need it most.

These effects of SOX's requirements on small firms, particularly the internal controls rule, mean that SOX is serving as an entry barrier to public ownership of business firms.

Cutting Off Information

SOX may not only increase firms' disclosure costs, but may also actually reduce the quantity and quality of disclosure in some respects.

Taking the Informed Out of the Loop. By reducing potential conflicts of interest, SOX also severs links that could provide

high-quality information. Most importantly, prohibitions on consulting work by auditors and the required periodic change of auditors reduce potential "knowledge spillovers" between auditing and
consulting and truncate the learning process in auditor-client relationships.[56] Similarly, at the director level, directors who have other
links with the firm might do a better job recognizing concerns that
might arise in audits and the tricks insiders might be playing, and
therefore may be more effective members of audit committees, than
directors who have "Caesar's wife" independence.

The SOX provision requiring lawyers to "report evidence of a
material violation of securities law or breach of fiduciary duty or
similar violation by the company or any agent thereof" obviously
inhibits conversations between lawyers and the firm's agents, as discussed above. Indeed, this issue was thoroughly debated in drafting
rule 1.13(b)–(c) of the American Bar Association's Model Rules of
Professional Conduct, which rejected a SOX-type approach. Rule
1.13(b) requires the lawyer to "proceed as is reasonably necessary in
the best interest of the organization," giving consideration to a variety
of factors. This language requires lawyers to exercise professional
judgment about reporting facts, and to consider a variety of different
actions. With SOX, however, Congress did not hesitate to change
radically the relationship between lawyers and their corporate clients.

The question in these situations is whether the benefits of higher-
quality information outweigh the costs of potential bad incentives.
The answer may vary from one situation to another, which suggests
that the one-size-fits-all SOX answer is inappropriate. For example,
the amount of information directors or auditors get from their other
links with the firm may depend on the complexity or unique prop-
erties of the firm's business. Also, the costs of potential incentive
problems may depend on the quality of monitoring the firm is getting from other sources. A fully independent audit committee may be
enough to ensure that the auditor is doing its job without also prohibiting the auditor from performing nonaudit services.

Reducing Trust. SOX also may reduce information flow between
employees by reducing trust and creating adversarial relationships

within the firm.[57] For example, a worker whose conduct was at least arguably innocent or defensible in the light of applicable rules, but did nevertheless hurt the firm, might reasonably fear punishment by overly zealous monitors or whistleblowers and therefore may be reluctant to communicate with them.

Insiders who are closely monitored may become less trustworthy. Some scholars think that legal sanctions "crowd out" the motivations people have to be trustworthy when they are not subject to these sanctions.[58] Also, the widespread dislike of what many corporate employees view as wasted effort and paperwork under SOX might make compliance a kind of game or adversarial process, and thereby discourage cooperation.

The trick, then, is to find the precise balance between sanctions that help ensure that insiders will not rely excessively on underlings, and sanctions that encourage underlings to be more untrustworthy. Again, this is best done on a firm-by-firm basis rather than by one-size-fits-all regulation. And it certainly cannot be done by the sort of rush to judgment that happened in the summer of 2002.

Inducing Cover-Ups. After insiders have committed acts for which they can be held liable, their interests may change from serving the firm's interest in protecting its reputation to serving their own interest in staying out of jail. Although a cover-up also may increase potential penalties, the insider may decide that he has a better chance of avoiding detection. Also, insiders who are facing jail may become less risk-averse and gamble everything on even a small chance of not getting caught.[59]

SOX increases these problems by imposing liability, including criminal liability, even on those who have not themselves engaged in self-aggrandizing conduct, but have certified reports where they had knowledge of internal controls lapses or failed to disclose information to auditors and the audit committee.

Although there is often a correlation between this conduct and more culpable wrongs, in some situations SOX may make criminals out of those who would otherwise be innocent. For example, section 302 requires officers to certify that they have disclosed to auditors "any fraud, whether or not material, that involves management or other employees who have a significant role in the issuer's internal controls." Suppose, for example, the officer took office supplies, or knows of an officer or accountant who did, in violation of company rules (perhaps imposed because of SOX). By not disclosing and certifying, the officer has committed a criminal offense, punishable under section 906 by up to ten years in jail. Given these provisions, in future cases executives might find themselves exposed to criminal and civil liability at the time of approving defective procedures, before they knew or could have known that the procedures were being used to perpetrate fraud. When they do find out about the fraud, their existing exposure may induce them to participate in a cover-up.

Perverse Incentives and Undoing Efficient Risk-Bearing

An important effect of SOX is to put an increased burden of the risk of corporate fraud on monitors and gatekeepers such as auditors, lawyers, outside directors, and senior executives. This is true not only of the liability provisions discussed above, but also of provisions like section 304, which requires reimbursement of compensation and stock profits following accounting misstatements, regardless of whether the executive knew of the fraud and even if he exercised all reasonable care in monitoring and instituting controls.

This is questionable policy. As discussed at the beginning of chapter 2, a significant function of the modern corporation is to reduce the costs of risk-bearing by enabling investors to own diversified portfolios of shares. For diversified shareholders, if one company goes down because of fraud, the portfolio is still largely intact. But SOX undoes this advantage by shifting enormous risk back to individuals. Under SOX, an executive who does not take every conceivable precaution against fraud exposes himself to the risk of a personal catastrophe. Even if the executive is protected from personal liability through indemnification or insurance, he may behave more cautiously than the shareholders would want to avoid the risk litigation poses to his reputation, which he cannot reduce by diversifying.[60]

Nor can the significant risk-shifting in SOX be justified on the ground that the defendants are better able to monitor or take precautions against fraud. In many situations there may be little an auditor or a lawyer effectively can do to prevent or spot fraud. Instead, they might order excessive precaution—more than the shareholders would want if they could make the decision— in order to protect themselves from the risk of ruinous liability. In other words, the same separation of ownership and control that leads to agent fraud also leads to excessive precautions against it. Instead of reducing agency costs, SOX may actually increase them.

Consider the ways that risk-averse executives may respond to the extra risk SOX imposes. They may avoid types of business or transactions that are particularly likely to trigger suspicion and liability in the event of fraud, even if these transactions maximize the value of the firm. These would include, for example, the derivatives and special-purpose entities that attracted so much attention in Enron but might have been valuable if properly managed. Or risk-averse executives may adjust disclosure so as to minimize liability but not necessarily increase accuracy. For example, they may use overly conservative accounting methods, or hedge or qualify disclosures.[61] This may reduce errors like those common in the pre-SOX era, but at the cost of introducing a different type of error. It will not necessarily increase market efficiency because market prices reflect basic asset values and expectations of future cash flows rather than accounting methods.

These incentives to avoid risk excessively might be offset by compensating executives in ways that make them act more like shareholders, such as with options or restricted shares.[62] Yet SOX moves in the opposite direction by banning some types of loans to executives, including loans for buying the company's stock. In this way, it simultaneously creates a problem and limits private contractual solutions to the problem.

Criminalization of Corporate Agency Costs

SOX is one of many examples of the recent trend toward using criminal sanctions to deter and punish social and commercial conduct that traditionally has been subject only to civil sanctions.[63] Although criminalization of all antisocial activities may be politically popular or expedient, there are numerous reasons for questioning the propriety of using such sanctions against many individual and corporate actions. For example, many regulatory crimes are strict liability crimes that do not require the traditional proof of criminal intent, *mens rea.*

SOX's most important criminal provisions are section 807, which increases the criminal penalty for knowingly committing securities fraud, including imprisonment for up to twenty-five years, and section 903, which increases imprisonment for mail and wire fraud from five to twenty years. Apart from increasing the penalties, SOX exacerbates the "over-criminalization" problems discussed above by enabling criminal liability even for those who have not themselves engaged in self-aggrandizing conduct, but have certified reports where they had knowledge of internal controls lapses or failed to disclose information to auditors and the audit committee. In this regard, it is worth noting that the new crimes added by SOX are on top of numerous other criminal sanctions—including the common-law fraud and federal securities laws—that are being used to prosecute former Enron executives Kenneth Lay and Jeffrey Skilling and others. The following discussion covers some of the general problems of corporate criminal liability that SOX makes even worse.

The Folly of Criminalizing Corporate Agency Costs. The challenge of controlling corporate agency costs is at the heart of corporate law and the contractual theory of the corporation. Senior executives and board members are expected to act on behalf of their shareholders. In addition to fiduciary duties under state corporation law, there are strong market incentives for officers and directors to act in their shareholders' best interests. Of course, because monitoring of executive performance is costly, there is always some opportunity for executives to behave in ways that do not maximize shareholder value. Such agency costs are a fact of corporate organization. Indeed, they are anticipated and reflected in market prices. The market rewards firms that do a better job of controlling agency costs.

If corporations do not control agency costs and maximize share value, several things that are not good for officers can happen. First, the corporation can become the target of a tender offer or proxy battle for control. Second, the corporation will not fare well in its product markets. It will lose market share and may ultimately go bankrupt. And, if agency costs are extraordinary, civil lawsuits may be brought against the board and officers.

Criminal sanctions for violating SOX may actually increase agency costs. A major concern of agency theory has been that corporate managers were not being diligent enough in pursuing their obligation to maximize the value of the firm. For example, managers could simply be lazy. Under SOX, laziness—failure to take the time to evaluate controls before attesting to their adequacy—can result in criminal liability. Although this threat should take care of the laziness part of agency costs, it might create a larger problem—instead of being lazy, managers might focus too many of the corporation's resources on ensuring the adequacy of corporate controls in order to avoid personal criminal liability. That is, in order to avoid criminal liability, the managers are likely to use corporate resources to their own benefit, even though they know it is not in the best interest of shareholders.

The analysis of criminal sanctions explains why corporate executives will tend to interpret section 404 compliance requirements strictly. As long as criminal liability is perceived as a consequence of failure to comply, overcompliance is going to be the norm.[64] The SEC's and PCAOB's suggestions in spring 2005 that auditors back off on their strict interpretations fell on deaf ears in part because criminal liability in a statute is much more powerful than a pep talk.[65]

Weakening the Moral Force of the Criminal Law. Criminal liability for internal controls lapses exacerbates an inherent problem with criminal liability in the corporate governance context: The criminal law loses both its moral force and moral legitimacy if it is used to discipline behavior that is not clearly distinguishable from innocent behavior or is not regarded by most people as culpable. Thus, even if manipulating corporate transactions to give a misleading picture of the firm is inefficient or morally wrong, it should not necessarily be criminal because it is often difficult to distinguish such behavior from innocent aggressive accounting. It is an even more serious problem if the defendant simply certified the adequacy of internal controls falsely, even if the defendant arguably knew that the precautions were inadequate.

SOX in the Context of Current Prosecutor Practices. SOX's criminal provisions should be analyzed in the context of how federal prosecutors will use their expanded powers to enforce these provisions.

First, SOX helps prosecutors use their broad discretion to coerce guilty pleas by threatening long prison sentences—now increased by SOX section 906—and offering the option of shorter sentences or civil fines. Plea-bargaining defendants then are available to testify against others in their firms. In SOX "internal controls" trials, the plea-bargaining defendants might testify not only about what their codefendants knew about the fraud, but also about circumstances bearing on what they should have known about the inadequacy of controls.[66]

Second, prosecutors are increasingly using their power and discretion to compromise corporate agents' ability to defend themselves against criminal charges by threatening their employers. Although SOX did not create this problem, it exacerbates it by expanding the scope of corporate criminal liability with which corporations and their agents can be charged. Thus, in the wake of SOX, federal prosecutors have more opportunity and leeway to use failure to cooperate with an investigation as a lever to obtain information. Suppose, for example, that a U.S. attorney begins an investigation into the possibility of executive wrongdoing, such as faulty certification of internal controls, perhaps alerted by a SOX-protected whistleblower. Prosecutors may demand that the corporation agree to waive the attorney-client privilege, and object to advancement of attorneys' fees to defendants. Under an explicit policy, the Justice Department may use the corporation's refusal to "cooperate" as a factor in deciding whether to charge the corporation with criminal violations that could threaten its ability to remain in business.[67] Indeed, KPMG succumbed to just such threats in order to avoid becoming the next Arthur Andersen.[68] Yet, without their employer's support, the employees may not be able to bear the huge costs of defending themselves against a taxpayer-supported government prosecution. At the American Bar Association's annual meeting in Chicago in August 2005, the ABA House of Delegates passed a resolution stating it "opposes the routine practice by government officials of seeking to obtain a waiver of attorney-client privilege or work product doctrine through the granting or denial of any benefit or advantage."[69]

Finally, information that has been pried from the company when either the company or its executives are under the threat of criminal prosecution, even if it does not lead to criminal convictions, may find its way into the hands of civil attorneys, who will then use it against the company.

Auditor Regulation

As detailed above, SOX imposes significant new regulation on auditing firms, including the creation of a new regulatory body with which auditors must register, the PCAOB, regulation of auditing standards, and restriction of ties with clients. This regulation may impose significant burdens on auditing firms. For example, auditors may need to protect themselves from liability or sanction by insisting on routinely checking every piece of information they receive from clients, even if the costs of this type of audit outweigh the benefits to investors in uncovering fraud. Remember that investors in publicly held corporations hold diversified portfolios, which makes it cheaper for them to bear risk than to put it on the auditing firms. Moreover, auditor checking may duplicate fraud protection from other sources, such as inside managers, lawyers, and outside directors.

Rules mandating auditors' financial independence by barring them from performing ancillary services for clients have been particularly contentious. Because of the auditor independence rules, a firm cannot use its own auditor to advise it on appropriate compliance methods. Rather, it has to use a consultant, which could be another auditing firm, who must compile information about the business from scratch, in order to help set up the system that the firm's auditor will now review. This additional expense for the company does not produce profits for most firms, since it is necessitated solely by the suspicion, unsupported by data, that nonaudit work for clients reduces audit quality.[70] But it is good for accounting firms, since the inefficiency adds to their profits even as it reduces those of the clients. So auditing firms get rich from a law that was intended in part to address their own failures. This regulation was the product of "policy entrepreneurs," particularly including former SEC chairman Arthur Levitt Jr., who strongly advocated it in congressional testimony while disregarding studies that might have reduced the persuasiveness of the testimony.[71]

An additional problem inherent to auditor regulation is that, if auditors must bear some of the risk of fraud or reporting errors, it may be harder or more costly for riskier firms, such as startups or innovative firms, to obtain the auditing they need in order to access the public markets. There have been reports that, following SOX, auditors are dropping clients that are "considered too small to be worth the extra work now required, as well as those judged too risky to work with under the new accounting rules."[72] Thus, a law intended to improve auditing has reduced its availability.

Regulation of Analyst Conflicts

Securities analysts are a crucial source of market efficiency, which is, in turn, an important way to spot fraud and evaluate firms' monitoring and reporting mechanisms. Analysts' links with the investment banking departments of their firms arguably compromise their independence. Section 501 of SOX provides for the adoption of SEC rules intended to address these conflicts. However, ties between analysts and investment bankers may produce information that is otherwise too costly to communicate because of legal restrictions on disclosure.[73] This regulation decreases information as it increases independence. Thus, the costs of this regulation are likely to exceed the benefits because, among other things, it reduces the effectiveness of market monitoring.

Crippling the "Genius" of American Corporate Law

As discussed in chapter 3, efficient corporate governance rules could evolve in response to Enron and other meltdowns in the absence of SOX through state competition to supply corporate law. Given the potential positive role of state competition in corporate governance reform, it is unfortunate that SOX moves in the opposite direction, toward an erosion of that role. There was once a fairly clear divide between federal law on disclosure and state law on substantive governance rules. The Supreme Court clearly endorsed this distinction in the *Santa Fe* case, which denied liability under the federal securities laws for conduct that was fully disclosed to shareholders.[74] However, since *Santa Fe*, Congress and the SEC have been moving toward greater federalization of corporate governance.

SOX represents a qualitative leap and a significant new threat to state corporate law. Specifically, the act makes numerous inroads into corporate governance issues formerly considered to be quintessentially subject to state control, unrelated to the kind of disclosure rules that were formerly the exclusive province of federal law. Among other things, SOX

- requires complete independence of audit committee directors, along the way providing a new federal definition of director independence;

- directly controls executive compensation by requiring some bonuses to be returned to the company and by prohibiting certain executive loans;

- determines the power of a board committee vis-à-vis the board as a whole, the shareholders, and the managers by requiring that the board's audit committee

control the hiring and firing of accountants and the
nonaudit work accountants do for the corporation;

- provides for specific SEC rules on off-balance-sheet
  transactions and special-purpose vehicles.

The problem of federal interference in state competition is not
simply a matter of the federal government ousting the states from
particular issues where federal supervision is deemed necessary,
such as takeovers in the Williams Act. Rather, the problem is that
each federal intervention in corporate governance law increases the
general federal presence, has spillover effects beyond the specific
federal rules adopted, and increases the threat of future intervention. These effects incrementally reduce both the scope and incentives for state action. As pieces of exclusive state jurisdiction fall
away, the states are increasingly constrained in applying a consistent policy framework to interrelated issues such as fiduciary duties
and board powers. Moreover, state legislatures and courts have
less incentive to undertake major policy initiatives in areas that
Congress and the SEC are occupying or seem likely to occupy soon.
In other words, entire areas of state lawmaking become "vestigial-
ized," as David Skeel showed has happened for governance of insol-
vent firms in the wake of federal bankruptcy law.[75] Thus, even if the
federal government were able to legislate more efficiently on a particular issue—and there is little reason to think it can after SOX—
the federal legislation may be inefficient, given its overall effect on
state policymaking in corporate governance.

The executive loans prohibition is especially problematic because it
departs so strikingly, not only from the disclosure orientation of federal law, but also from the state law approach of leaving these issues to
shareholder and manager voting. It also replaces an active state evolu-
tion in this area that has produced several distinct approaches from
which firms can choose.[76] As Delaware Chancellor William B.
Chandler III and vice chancellor Leo E. Strine Jr. have written,

By this method, Congress took upon itself responsibility
for delimiting the range of permissible transactions that

corporations chartered by state law could consummate. In itself, the mandate is relatively trivial, but its precedential significance may not be. What's next? A ban on going private transactions? Or on options-based compensation of executives? Or on interested transactions?[77]

Moreover, apart from the areas of specific invasion of substantive rules, the internal controls reports under SOX section 404 invade a developing area of state law on directors' duties to ensure that

> information and reporting systems exist in the organization that are reasonably designed to provide to senior management and to the board itself timely, accurate information sufficient to allow management and the board, each within its scope, to reach informed judgments concerning both the corporation's compliance with law and its business performance.[78]

Although most Delaware corporations have taken advantage of a Delaware statutory provision to waive the duty of care, which would implicate this duty, Delaware courts have been developing a "good faith" duty that theoretically could embrace a duty to develop information and reporting systems. Alternatively, the Delaware legislature could decide explicitly to adopt a nonwaivable duty in the wake of Enron. But SOX effectively precludes these state law alternatives.

The costs of the creeping federalization of corporate governance include the ousting of the expert Delaware courts from the ability to develop detailed policy on a case-by-case basis, and the loss of the opportunity states offer for proposing a variety of approaches to difficult governance issues. Chandler and Strine note that SOX and other reforms adopted in 2002 following Enron substituted a rigid, one-size-fits-all federal approach for Delaware's "principles-based" approach:

> The Delaware approach has tended to create incentives for particular good governance practices, yet also recognizes

that what generally works for most boards may not be the best method for some others. The fiduciary duty form of accountability is well-suited to this sort of flexibility because it is context-specific in application. But because the 2002 Reforms naturally take a more rule-based form, they come with the risk of codifying (by statute or contract) an array of procedures that, when implemented in their totality, might be less than optimal.[79]

The different approaches of federal and state law sometimes may force a collision. For example, in *Newcastle Partners L. P. v. Vesta Insurance Group Inc.*, the Delaware Court of Chancery refused to allow the company to delay its annual meeting to give its accounting firm time to supply audited statements required by the SEC. The court said,

> There are, of course, some circumstances in which a state's governance of internal corporate affairs is preempted by federal law, but those instances are rare, and occur only when the law of the state of incorporation is "inconsistent with a national policy on foreign or interstate commerce."[80]

As federal law makes further inroads into state governance law, these confrontations are likely to become more frequent.

The conflicts threaten to impose a federal perspective on corporate governance, in sharp contrast to the perspective that has emerged from decades of lawmaking in Delaware and other states. Thus, in contrasting the emphasis of Congress and the SEC on the "ordinary investor" with Delaware's more realistic understanding of the important role of institutional shareholders, Delaware chief justice Myron Steele has said that

> increasingly institutional shareholders dominate the market. Do they need an advocate in DC wedded to prescriptive regulation or can their complaints, if any,

be as readily and more equitably addressed by private ordering in State civil law litigation on a case by case contextual environment? Moving corporate governance to DC means increased costs with little effort to determine benefit, an arena for dispute resolution decisionmaking that is not unbiased and portends no guarantee that the guidelines, regs or pronouncements from the banks of the Potomac will enhance long term shareholder value. Those who advocate a drift from the common law resolution of disputes by a highly trained and experienced cadre of jurists to the bureaucracy in DC should be careful what they wish for.[81]

More often than direct confrontation, federal law will cause subtle changes in state law, or make this law more indeterminate. For example, the SOX approach, particularly including its rules on director independence, apparently has had the effect of destabilizing Delaware law. Vice Chancellor Strine predicted immediately after SOX was passed that federal law would pressure state courts to consider personal, social, and professional relationships in assessing director independence.[82] One writer documented state decisions citing SOX, noting that during 2003, the Delaware Supreme Court sharply increased both the number of reversals of chancery court rulings and results favoring plaintiff shareholders.[83] Another discussed how the chancery court, apparently responding to SOX, expanded the state definition of director interest to move closer to the federal standard, though the supreme court apparently limited this to the sensitive context of special litigation committees.[84]

Of particular interest in this respect is SOX's apparent effect on the shifting results in the Disney litigation involving Michael Ovitz's employment contract and termination. Prior to SOX, the Delaware courts had dismissed a shareholder complaint against the Disney board.[85] On remand, following SOX, Chancellor Chandler refused to dismiss the amended complaint.[86] But then, two years later, after a lengthy trial, Chandler denied all relief.[87] To be sure, the shifts were not clearly attributable to SOX.[88] However, it is reasonable to infer that these shifting outcomes in the same highly publicized case were at least partly attributable to the Delaware courts' concerns about further corporate law in the wake of SOX.

To the extent that federal law is causing a shift in the Delaware law on director independence, and even apart from the problems inherent in decreeing a single norm from Washington, this shift is likely in the wrong direction. Chandler and Strine note that SOX forbids a director affiliated with a substantial shareholder to serve on the audit committee. They point out that this restriction may apply to the representatives of venture capital or leveraged buyout firms:

> This incentive system is contrary to much good thinking in academia and in Delaware decisional law, both of which have taken the view that independent directors who have a substantial stake as common stockholders in the company's success are better motivated to diligently and faithfully oversee management.[89]

The judges are also concerned that, as the federal prohibition on ties with officers creeps into state law, it

> could have an unfair effect if extended into the litigation context without appropriate sensitivity. There may well be situations in which the CEO of a company is entirely capable of acting "independently" on an issue because his management status (and presumed desire to keep it) has no bearing at all on his incentives. . . . Well-qualified people may be dissuaded from serving on boards, to the resulting detriment of stockholders.[90]

In short, SOX could have significant negative effects in eroding the competition among the states to supply corporation law—what Roberta Romano has called the "genius" of our corporate law system.[91] The effect cannot be blinked away by arguing that SOX's interference with state law is only on specific issues. This federal intrusion, when coupled with the federalization that had preceded

SOX and the threat SOX poses for the future, could seriously weaken the viability of state corporation law. SOX harms a major institutional framework that has generated effective corporate governance for over one hundred years. Combined with the discussion of its manifest defects, there is strong reason to believe that the costs of SOX's adverse effect on the development of state law outweigh any benefits of an increased federal presence in this area.

Chasing Away Foreign Firms

The effect of SOX on issuers not based in the United States is a classic example of the nonobvious, and even unintended, consequences of the act. Its application to non-U.S. firms was not debated and scarcely mentioned during Congress's brief deliberations. Yet SOX's new substantive governance standards and liabilities impose especially high costs on foreign firms trading in the United States.

The most attention has been given to the SOX requirements for independent audit committees. The SEC rules interpreting this provision exclude from the audit committee any "affiliated person," defined as one who "controls, or is controlled by, or is under common control with, such issuer."[92] This is a problem for the vast majority of non-U.S. firms that are controlled by one or a few large shareholders.[93] The act is particularly problematic for firms subject to the laws of Germany and other countries that require two-level boards consisting of a managerial unit and a supervisory unit. German companies with two-level boards appoint the auditor at the shareholders' annual general meeting, upon nomination and determination of the auditor's independence by the supervisory board.[94] Thus, complying with SOX may conflict with the shareholders' appointment power under German law. SOX's excludes anyone who receives a "consulting, advisory or other compensatory fee from the issuer" or is "an affiliated person" of the issuer,[95] which may include most labor members of the German supervisory board. And SOX may exclude others who have relationships with the company, including representatives of banks and other large shareholders who have significant monitoring functions in German firms.

Other SOX provisions may conflict with foreign firms' home-country law. Just as its executive loan prohibition goes further than many state laws, it also conflicts with foreign laws, such as German law, which permits loans approved by the supervisory board. Also, SOX requirements for executive certification of reports and supervision of internal controls, as well as other rules imposing liability on executives and requiring return of executive compensation paid during restatements, may conflict with laws in other countries, such as Japan, that provide for hierarchies different from the simple triangle in U.S. firms. Not only might it be difficult to identify which people the act covers, but SOX provisions may be inappropriate in these countries because executives are less powerful and less in need of policing.[96] Also, SOX provisions requiring monitoring by and independence of lawyers and other professionals may not make sense in countries where the professionals lack independence from clients. Indeed, SOX's entire scheme for regulating the internal governance of firms may make little sense in firms that rely on monitoring by large shareholders rather than fiduciary duties and other regulation.

The differences between SOX and foreign law may arise unexpectedly. For example, the SOX whistleblowing provisions, which provide for anonymous tips, may conflict with European privacy laws.[97] U.S. companies operating in Europe may be forced either to comply with SOX or to comply with local law. Even worse, European Union data-protection laws are applied differently in each of the EU's twenty-five countries, making it even harder for U.S. companies to comply with SOX.

SOX, therefore, imposes significant costs on the non-U.S. firms to which it applies.[98] This includes not only firms that have elected to trade in the United States, but subsidiaries of U.S. firms.

The anecdotal evidence shows that SOX is taking a toll on the trading of foreign securities here. For example, John Thain, CEO of the New York Stock Exchange, reported that for two years after SOX was passed, new cross-listings fell to half the annual totals prior to the act. New York's share of new stock offerings of foreign companies dropped from 90 percent in 2000 to 10 percent in 2005, in large part because of the high costs SOX imposes on foreign firms.[99] Meanwhile, London is pressing its regulatory advantage by offering a special low-cost market (AIM) for smaller companies just as the United States, through SOX, is raising costs for these firms.[100]

The reduced presence of foreign firms in the United States causes significant problems in the U.S. market. These include both reduced income to the U.S. securities industry and reduced access of U.S. investors to foreign firms, because of the higher costs of trading foreign firms on foreign markets. This phenomenon is hurting the "ordinary investors" about whom Congress and the SEC always purport to worry, since professionals can always buy shares in London.

SOX's defenders initially relied on the idea that there were no hard data on the effects of SOX on foreign firms and cross-listings, and the inconclusive fact that firms were continuing to cross-list in the United States.[101] However, harder evidence of SOX's effect on foreign firms has now become available. Kate Litvak has shown that stock prices of foreign companies cross-listed in the United States declined during key announcements indicating the act's application to foreign issuers, and increased in reaction to announcements qualifying application of the act. These reactions were strongest for European companies and companies from high-GDP countries—that is, firms from a relatively high-quality institutional environment.[102] Litvak controls for economic and political factors by, among other things, comparing companies within a given country that are, and are not, cross-listed.

Not surprisingly in light of these facts, non-U.S. firms complained loudly soon after SOX was passed. From the beginning there has been some concern that SOX would threaten cross-listings.[103] Foreign firms have continued to react, particularly to the SOX internal controls certification. Some firms, spurred by the approaching application of this rule, want an exemption for foreign firms that have less than five percent of their share volume trading in the United States, rather than the three-hundred-shareholder rule that now applies.[104]

The effect of SOX on non-U.S. firms has triggered a political dynamic that may have far-reaching consequences. This began when the United States responded to criticisms from German and other companies by issuing a rule that partially exempts foreign firms from some SOX requirements.[105] The rule, among other things, permits nonexecutive employees in foreign-based issuers to serve as audit committee members, large shareholders to send observer representatives, and foreign firms to substitute for the audit committee a board of auditors or similar body whose independence and responsibility for appointing and overseeing the firm's auditor is provided for in home-country legal or listing provisions.[106] Also, the SEC has clarified that the SOX prohibition on trading during pension blackouts applies only to foreign firms' principal executive, financial, and accounting officers;[107] that lawyers' duties under SOX do not apply to foreign attorneys who are not admitted in the United States and do not advise clients regarding U.S. law;[108] and that the SEC has delayed until 2006 the application of internal controls reporting to foreign firms.[109]

These rules raise the question of how far the SEC can go in exempting foreign firms before triggering significant complaints from their U.S. competitors in the U.S. capital markets. The exemptions undoubtedly are attributable to some extent to the fact that foreign firms are much better able to exit the U.S. market than U.S.-based firms. The latter may be subject to U.S. laws even if they trade overseas, and they have other business reasons for needing to trade in the United States. To the extent the exemptions are, or should be, based on the costs of compliance, they arguably should apply to any firm that is incorporated under and must comply with the corporate law of another country, regardless of where the corporation's operations are based. But any such exemption would invite U.S. firms to avoid U.S. law by incorporating elsewhere. To the extent that such competition forces U.S. regulators and legislators to reassess the damage they have done to American securities markets, such exits by U.S. firms could ultimately help correct the SOX mistake.

5

The Litigation Time Bomb

SOX's defenders say that the main problem with SOX is the cost of filling out forms, that for big firms this is mainly a startup cost that will be fixed as firms adjust, that the SEC can fix the bigger problem for small firms by exemptions or modifications of the rules, and that the remaining costs are outweighed by the benefits. As discussed in the preceding chapter, this is unduly sanguine. Even from a paperwork perspective, SOX threatens to cause a major restructuring in how firms do business. The problems become even more serious if one considers SOX from the perspective of the litigation it will trigger a few years out.

This chapter explains that a SOX litigation "time bomb" will explode with the next major stock market adjustment because SOX not only provides new causes of action; it also appears to make proving liability relatively easy by tracing the decline in market price to some inadequacy in internal controls. Similarly, SOX litigation "time bomblets" will be triggered whenever a specific industry or sector suffers a downturn. Shareholder litigation on this scale should not be confused with investor protection.

A Review of Liability Threats under SOX

The biggest liability threats under SOX arise under sections 302 and 906. As detailed above, section 302 requires officers to certify not only the accuracy of the financial statement, as they were required to do even before SOX, but also that they have

- designed "internal controls" that ensure material information is "made known" to the officers;

- evaluated and presented their conclusions as to the effectiveness of these controls as of at least ninety days prior to the report;

- disclosed to the firm's auditors and board audit committee "significant deficiencies" in the design of the controls that could affect processing and reporting of financial data;

- identified for the auditors "material weaknesses in internal controls" and "any fraud, whether or not material" involving employees "who have a significant role in the issuer's internal controls";

- indicated "significant changes in internal controls or in other factors that could significantly affect internal controls" since the last evaluation.

The SEC has further articulated executives' internal controls reporting obligations. According to the SEC

> The assessment of a company's internal controls over financial reporting must be based on procedures sufficient both to evaluate its design and to test its operating effectiveness. Controls subject to such assessment include, but are not limited to controls . . . related to the prevention, identification, and detection of fraud. The nature of a company's testing activities will largely depend on the circumstances of the company and the significance of the control. However, inquiry alone generally will not provide an adequate basis for management's assessment.[1]

As discussed above, the assessment "must be supported by . . . documentation, regarding both the design of internal controls and the testing processes."

Violation of these provisions is treated the same as violations of other securities law provisions.[2] That would include private class-action suits under the general antifraud provisions of the securities laws, including section 10(b) of the Securities and Exchange Act of 1934 and rule 10b-5, for false certifications. The SEC has already indicated the potential for personal liability for false certifications in an administrative proceeding against Richard Scrushy, former CEO of HealthSouth, and the firm he founded, for false certifications under the requirements of pre-SOX law.[3] This case illustrates that the concept of executive certification of reports is not new to SOX. What SOX added is the potential for liability, not only for knowing of untruths as to the actual numbers, which is what the SEC claimed against Scrushy, but also for knowing about bad processes that ended up producing bad numbers. SOX section 906 includes the bracing addition of criminal penalties of up to a fine of a million dollars and ten years in prison for one who certifies under this section "knowing" that the periodic report does not comply with the section's requirement, or five million dollars and twenty years for "willfully" certifying with this knowledge.[4]

Using 20/20 Hindsight to Assess Risk

SOX cases will turn on whether a problem (almost certainly a precipitous drop in share price) occurred because of a "significant" deficiency or "material weakness" in controls that the executives should have reported to the auditors, or because of a gap in an internal controls system that the executives had assessed in the certified report as adequate. SOX takes care of the case in which senior executives arguably build a wall between themselves and the fraudsters deliberately. But there are serious problems with applying these standards where the executives have not been deliberately fraudulent. To begin with, as Harvey Pitt has pointed out, even a tiny possibility that a flaw in the system could permit a very serious event such as destruction of the company could be "material," taking into account the magnitude of the potential problem.[5] There is also a question of which "controls . . . related to the prevention, identification, and detection of fraud" will be deemed to have been necessary to prevent the new kinds of fraud arising in future cases, particularly if the fraud originates deep in the organization.[6]

Even if courts and the SEC are ultimately reasonable in applying these provisions, their reasonableness might come only after considerable litigation expense. As Pitt observes:

> In a litigation following the discovery of an error and using 100 percent hindsight, the plaintiff's attorney isn't going to draw any distinction between probability and fact. As a result, a one-in-one-thousand event and incidents of higher probability are treated the same. Management must deal with both with the same degree of response. This creates considerable uncertainty for accountants during an audit and leads them to stress caution at the expense of cost.[7]

One might argue that SOX prevents excessive liability by requiring only that the certifiers know of weaknesses or deficiencies in internal controls. This "scienter" requirement might work, at least to some extent, if the question were whether the managers knew of the fraud. But, as emphasized above, SOX moves the culpability back a step, to whether the executives knew of deficiencies in the procedures for spotting fraud. The managers may well have known at the relevant time about a particular characteristic of the internal controls system that they assessed as adequate, and even that this characteristic might fail to spot fraud under some circumstances, but not that this gap was a sufficient problem that it needed to be rectified, or that it was a "significant" deficiency that needed to be identified for the auditors.

SOX is likely also to lead to litigation under state fiduciary law, either on the basis that federal law affects the application of state duties, as by defining director independence, or through a claim that violation of the act injured the firm.[8] Moreover, as violations of law, these claims arguably would be nonwaivable under Delaware law.[9]

Litigators' Incentives

Since, as we have seen, these new provisions eliminate the trouble-some need to prove knowledge of actual fraud, civil trial lawyers and government attorneys have strong incentives to bring cases under them. The trial lawyers do not necessarily have the interests of shareholders or investors in mind, since risk-averse defendants (officers and directors) face incentives to settle even dubious cases, particularly if their indemnification or insurance depends on an unfavorable outcome.

One can hope that courts will filter out the worst cases, particu-larly by dismissing them on the pleadings or other preliminary stage. But courts face the perennial problem of the hindsight bias. To be sure, courts appear to be dealing with this problem by expressing a reluctance to find what they have called "fraud by hindsight." But, as Gulati, Rachlinski, and Langevoort have shown, the cases applying this approach actually are using the rationale to justify management of what they subjectively conclude are weak cases, without dealing realistically with the underlying bias problem.[10] Thus, there is no rea-son to believe that this doctrine, developed for the specific context of determining the existence of fraud, will be adequate to deal with the new issue under SOX of whether senior executives wrongfully certi-fied the processes for preventing fraud. Even courts that are suppos-edly wary of fraud by hindsight may well impose liability for precaution by hindsight—that is, the failure to protect *ex ante* against frauds that have become obvious only later.

It may be that courts will impose civil and criminal liability for SOX violations only against corporate thieves and defrauders, as in past cases. If so, these problems may not be serious. But that is to say that SOX is not pernicious only if it is ineffective.

The Potential for Blackmail

SOX creates an ideal scenario for "litigation blackmail," in the sense of inducing settlements for more than the value of the claim, because individual officers and directors face the threat of heavy discovery costs and potentially ruinous liability. This is particularly serious in light of the fact that, even before detonation of the SOX time bomb, securities class action settlements rose on an inflation-adjusted basis from $150 million in 1997 to $9.6 billion in 2005, with the average settlement size increasing sevenfold during this period, despite the enactment in 1995 of the Private Securities Litigation Reform Act intended to rein in securities class actions.[11]

The increased likelihood of blackmail is evident from several characteristics of post-SOX litigation. First, the event triggering litigation is likely to be a large and public loss of shareholder wealth, providing an opportunity for exaggerated damage claims. Plaintiffs may be able to bring "fraud-on-the-market" claims, in which all investors who traded during the period in which facts were not disclosed can recover the difference between the price at which they traded and the value as measured by the price adjustment when the facts were disclosed.[12] The damages are highly likely to exceed any realistic estimate of the loss by shareholders as a whole because, among other things, it is rarely clear how much of the price adjustment on disclosure can be attributed to the misrepresentation, and the damages are not offset by the gains of the investors with whom the plaintiffs traded.[13] Moreover, damages based on the price decline following disclosure might be significantly increased by a sort of feedback loop—the risk of litigation over the disclosure itself increases the price decline.[14]

Second, liability may turn not only on outright theft or lying about basic facts, but on whether executives certifying the firm's disclosures should have known about certain risks and the need for controls to deal with them.

Third, to the extent that plaintiffs sue both managers and the corporation itself, the actions may harm even some of the investors on whose behalf the action is brought, to the extent they are shareholders in the defendant corporation. The significant risk of liability and the potential for extravagant damages may induce managers to enter into settlements on behalf of the corporation that are not in the shareholders' interests. Since plaintiffs have little information about the facts when the complaint is filed, defendants can be expected to win most cases. Diversified shareholders therefore would prefer to settle very few cases; they are willing to take the risk of the occasional loss, particularly since the corporations in their portfolios will be plaintiffs about as often as they will be defendants. Individual defendants, on the other hand, stand a chance of losing everything in every case, and therefore have a strong incentive to settle, particularly if settlements (but not adjudications of liability) are covered by indemnification or insurance.

Fourth, litigation may cause significant distraction, as executives and staff must prepare for trial and comply with burdensome discovery requests. These costs are part of the calculus executives must take into account when deciding whether settling even a weak lawsuit is in the company's interest. Moreover, executives have an extra incentive to settle lawsuits to avoid the personal stress and embarrassment of litigation.

What Can Shareholders Do about the Time Bomb?

Although the litigation time bomb is ticking loudly enough for anybody to hear, there is not much shareholders can do to avoid it. Although shareholders can minimize the risk of managerial malfeasance, they cannot diversify away firms' compliance costs. Although firms have varying risks of fraud, the risk of SOX litigation forces all firms—good and bad—to incur excessive compliance costs. For this reason, rational shareholders would probably rather take their chances with good old-fashioned fraud and theft than the litigation lottery created by SOX.

6

The Bottom Line: Has SOX Been Worth It?

SOX's defenders claim that, despite all of the havoc the act has wrought, it has been worth the cost for curtailing the terrible frauds that led to it. We have shown that much of this could have been accomplished without federal intervention, and that SOX's costs have been more subtle and extensive than its defenders have suggested. This chapter discusses what we know so far about whether SOX's supposed benefits outweigh its costs.

Since SOX, several studies have shown its overall effects. The most direct evidence is the effect of its enactment on firms' market value. These studies, several of which were analyzed by Romano, generally indicate that the market has reacted negatively to the adoption and implementation of SOX, though the results are inconclusive because it is difficult to infer causation when the law affects every stock in the market.[1]

The most extensive and persuasive study of SOX's costs estimated the loss in total market value of firms around legislative events leading to the passage of SOX at $1.4 trillion.[2] The study specifically found that the market reacted negatively to the restriction of the provision of nonaudit services, provisions relating to corporate governance, and the internal controls provision. Firms with "weak" governance declined as the likelihood of passing tough SOX rules increased, indicating that investors thought the costs of such rules to poorly governed firms would exceed the benefits. In other words, if SOX were effective in protecting shareholders, then the market prices of firms with weak governance would have increased with its passage. Instead, the prices declined, suggesting that SOX does not protect even the investors in poorly governed corporations.

An earlier study showed that enactment of SOX was associated with positive stock returns.[3] Also, the study found no significant differences between SOX's effects on firms that had been managing earnings or had fully independent audit committees, and those on firms that had not. This indicates that the market did not expect SOX reforms in these areas to be meaningful.

Another study found that the SOX governance rules had a positive effect on the value of large firms, but no significant effect on small firms.[4] A third found that events "favorable" to SOX's enactment were associated with positive stock returns, but that firms that were better governed before the act did better after SOX.[5] This is generally consistent with the distinction between well and poorly governed firms in the first study discussed above. It is not clear what it means, however, since the better-governed firms arguably had both lower compliance costs and lower benefits from the SOX reforms. So the numbers could just mean that the firms that were already paying a lot for governance did better after SOX than their previously more efficiently managed rivals, who were now forced to incur higher costs.

All of these studies are highly sensitive to the events selected for measuring stock price effects. The studies that find positive returns associated with events favorable to SOX enactment include a period of rising stock prices that occurred after the market passage of SOX had been assured, and therefore probably after the market had registered the act's effects. By contrast, the study that finds significant negative stock price effects more realistically focuses on an earlier period of sharp market declines around the time when events such as President Bush's July 9 call for strong legislation made it evident that strong legislation would pass.

There is also evidence of positive market-price reaction to the SOX executive certification requirement.[6] Another study shows that firms' share prices did not react to certification, suggesting that the market could separate good from bad firms without certification.[7] Romano analyzes two of the studies in detail and concludes it is difficult to draw "any definitive conclusion" from them.[8]

There are several reasons to have serious doubts about whether SOX can be worth these high costs. First, there is evidence that the market simply does not care that much about the information SOX is extracting at such high costs. A study has found that firms disclosing internal controls weaknesses have a slightly higher cost of equity, but that this difference is mainly associated with general economic characteristics of the disclosing firms, except for a few that delayed their SOX 404 disclosures.[9] Further studies of this sort may provide additional information about the impact of the disclosures.

Second, there is the serious question whether the disclosures will have their intended effect of preventing fraud. For example, the recent Refco bankruptcy unfolded after disclosure that its CEO owed the firm $430 million. Neither SOX nor the intensive disclosure required in an initial public offering could protect investors. The prospectus did not disclose that the company's "receivables" were owed by its CEO or other "related party," since the identity of the debtor was disguised by cycling the loan through a customer.[10] The lesson is that all the disclosure in the world, including the detailed disclosures SOX requires of internal controls, cannot prevent fraud, even in a relatively small organization. And if businesspeople were not deterred from willful fraud prior to SOX by the risk of long jail sentences or fines under prior law, increasing the terms, raising the penalties, and extending the scope of liability to include failure to prevent fraud will not accomplish this, either. These changes are more likely to deter honest people from engaging in risky but productive businesses than they are to prevent dishonest people from circumventing the law.

Third, even if SOX elicits information that is valuable to rational and informed investors, it is unrealistic to expect that this will prevent another Enron-type bubble. During the boom that led to SOX, even sophisticated investors ignored ample warnings, such as the fact that WorldCom was repeatedly meeting its projections to the penny. They also ignored the warning of a hedge-fund manager that Enron had become a derivatives speculator with unhedged investments.[11] They bid Enron up to fantastic price-earnings multiples despite the obvious risk that its business, even if legitimate, was very vulnerable to competition. Investors were susceptible to confirmation and conservatism biases that led them to discount evidence inconsistent with the sky-high expectations engendered by the long-running bubble market.[12] More information alone cannot prevent these judgment errors. Even if it were possible to pound investors until they understood the risk, this might just drive them in the opposite, equally unrealistic, direction, particularly in bear markets.

In short, all of the mountains of information and inconvenience produced by SOX cannot prevent another Enron. The only thing that might have some effect is for investors to be more knowledgeable, careful, and skeptical, and to learn from their mistakes. As will be discussed in chapter 8, investor education holds out some hope. But SOX moves in the opposite direction, towards miseducation, by offering the false hope that Congress and the SEC have found the magic bullet that prevents fraud.

7

Immediate Policy Implications

The preceding analysis supports the overwhelming conclusion that SOX was a colossal mistake. By any reasonable standards of public policy analysis, the act should be repealed. In a recent survey, 58 percent of corporate directors in the United States favored repealing or overhauling SOX.[1] However, despite the mounting evidence and criticism, repeal is highly unlikely. Even if society is losing, the act retains the support of influential interest groups and the press. The big losers, such as entrepreneurs, are less organized and therefore less influential.

There is, however, a possible avenue to change. A favorable court decision in a recently filed lawsuit could provide the leverage to enact some major changes in SOX. On February 8, 2006, the Free Enterprise Fund filed a lawsuit alleging that the PCAOB violates the appointments clause of the Constitution because its members need to be appointed by the president or heads of executive branch departments rather than the SEC.[2] This suit has the potential to overturn all of SOX, which lacks a severability clause. If the plaintiff prevails, however, the courts are likely to give Congress a window of opportunity to fix the act. Although political reality makes it unlikely Congress will repeal SOX, lawmakers may be able to seize the opportunity to fix the act's worst flaws.

It is, therefore, worth discussing the changes Congress should consider if it has the opportunity or inclination. These changes might turn SOX from a debacle into a model for future federal regulation, along the lines of suggestions we will offer in chapter 8. Although some changes could be adopted by the SEC—and, indeed, Congress could be expected to delegate significant authority to the SEC—the SEC needs Congress to authorize and guide significant revisions.[3] Indeed, it is not even clear that the SEC has the authority under current law to adopt the changes it is considering.[4]

Defuse the Litigation Time Bomb

As detailed in chapter 5, SOX created a litigation time bomb that will explode with the next major market downturn. All of the perverse incentives of SOX are exacerbated by this threat. Congress can prevent this by amending the act to provide that violations of SOX cannot be redressed by private lawsuits.

Congress has acted before to curb excessive litigation against corporations. For example, in 1995, Congress passed the Private Securities Litigation Reform Act, which attempted to curb abuses in securities class action litigation by eliminating so-called "professional plaintiffs" and instituting pleading standards that were more stringent. In 2005, Congress passed the Class Action Fairness Act, which attempted to control forum-shopping in favorable "magnet" state courts by permitting removal of many class actions to federal courts.[5]

In support of an amendment addressing the litigation risk from SOX, Congress can cite language in the Supreme Court's recent *Dura* opinion.[6] The Court noted:

> Allowing a plaintiff to forgo giving any indication of the economic loss and proximate cause that the plaintiff has in mind would bring about harm of the very sort the statutes seek to avoid. . . . It would permit a plaintiff "with a largely groundless claim to simply take up the time of a number of other people, with the right to do so representing an in terrorem increment of the settlement value, rather than a reasonably founded hope that the [discovery] process will reveal relevant evidence." *Blue Chip Stamps*, 421 U.S., at 741, 95 S.Ct. 1917. Such a rule would tend to transform a private securities action into a partial downside insurance policy.[7]

Thus, removing the litigation time bomb—a modest, but very important, reform of SOX—may have significant political and legal traction.

Allow Opt-Outs or Opt-Ins

Congress demonstrated in SOX that it simply could not foresee the full effects of sweeping corporate reforms. This is an important reason corporate governance has generally been controlled by state, rather than federal, law. If a state makes a mistake, firms can, in effect, opt out by reincorporating in another state. If Congress makes a mistake, firms can avoid it only by the far more costly route of moving their activities and capital-raising offshore. This suggests that Congress might minimize the risk of imposing unanticipated costs—that is, the costs of miscalculating the impact of its regulation—by permitting firms to opt into or opt out of at least some of SOX's provisions. Leading candidates for opt-out would be the section 404 internal controls provision and the section 402 prohibition on executive loans.

The argument against opt-out is that this is contrary to the rationale for regulating disclosure through mandatory federal laws. Investors arguably need a certain minimum amount of information to make investment choices, including choices based on applicable governance rules. So, the argument goes, shareholder choice does not work for the very rules that make this choice effective. A problem with this argument, however, is that investors would not be making this choice about disclosure in the dark; they would know, at least, that they would be making a riskier investment because of what the firm may choose not to tell them. Indeed, risk-averse investors might tend to place an unrealistically high weight on this consideration, thereby giving firms an incentive to opt for disclosure. There are more sophisticated arguments for mandatory disclosure, but they do not tell us precisely what disclosures should be required.[8]

Two considerations support making some provisions of SOX, including those noted above, optional. First, as emphasized throughout this monograph, the optimal amount of fraud is not zero. At some point, regulation of fraud and disclosure is so costly that it is inefficient. The question is, who should decide when that is the case? Even if some mandatory disclosure is efficient, there may be significant debate at the margins. In these situations, it makes sense to let the shareholders decide. The debate raging over the internal controls disclosures indicates that this should be one of the marginal provisions for which opt-out is appropriate. Moreover, this public debate highlights for the shareholders both the costs and benefits of opting out of this particular disclosure provision.

Second, it is important to keep in mind that what is most significant about SOX is the way it veers off from the federal government's traditional concern with disclosure and into the sort of substantive governance provisions that traditionally have been the province of state corporate law. This is certainly true of the executive loan provision. It is also arguably true of some ostensibly disclosure-oriented provisions, like the internal controls provision, that effectively regulate governance. While the provision says only that the firm must disclose internal controls problems, in substance it not only strongly encourages firms to have controls, but effectively requires them to set up an internal framework that enables them to make the disclosure. This is regulation of governance and not merely of disclosure. In at least these cases, and probably others, shareholders should have the same opportunity they have under state law to decide the terms of their investments.

The specific mechanism for opt-out or opt-in could be the very proxy framework that Congress has approved as the basis for enabling shareholder choice. Thus, directors could propose the option in the proxy materials, and would be required by the proxy rules to give full disclosure of the reasons for and consequences of the proposal. Alternatively, shareholders could make an opt-in or opt-out proposal either by sending out their own proxy materials, or by taking advantage of the shareholder proposal rule.[9]

There are additional questions whether any options should be provisions that apply by default unless the firm opts out or that apply only if the firm opts in; the specific procedural requirements for opt-out or opt-in; which provisions would be subject to opt-out or opt-in; and which companies would have the options. Congress might delegate some of these questions to the SEC, to be determined through rulemaking after notice and comment.[10]

Foreign Firms

Prior to the Enron and WorldCom imbroglios, American capital markets were widely considered the strongest in the world. As discussed in chapter 4, SOX has made American markets less attractive to foreign companies, in part by imposing substantive governance provisions that conflict with these firms' home-country laws. This has provided a significant competitive opening for other securities markets, particularly London.

Congress can address this problem by exempting foreign firms either from SOX generally or from specific provisions, such as the audit committee and internal controls provisions that are so troublesome for many foreign firms. Alternatively, assuming Congress does not make these provisions or the act itself optional for all firms, it can make them optional for foreign firms. This might be the best approach, since some cross-listing foreign firms might actually prefer to "bond" their disclosures by subjecting themselves to the highest level of U.S. regulation.[11]

A potential problem with SOX exemptions and opt-outs for foreign firms is that they might give a significant advantage to the foreign firms over their U.S. competitors, particularly given the high costs of SOX discussed throughout this monograph. One response is that the different treatment is justified on the ground that foreign firms are subject to regulation in their home countries. But U.S. firms might protest that this regulation is weaker—at least it does not include SOX.

This problem might be dealt with by extending the exemption or the opt-out to any firm that is subject to the governance law of another country, irrespective of where it is physically based. Under current rules, whether a firm is subject to U.S. regulation depends on both where the firm is incorporated and organized and where its business, shareholders, and management are located.[12] This would appropriately reflect the key reason for exempting foreign firms. In other words, this change to SOX, while specifically responding to the need to treat U.S. and foreign firms comparably, might be a modest beginning toward recognizing a true regime of jurisdictional choice.[13]

Exempt Small Corporations

As discussed in chapter 4, SOX presents significant problems for small firms, since their compliance cost per dollar of capitalization is much higher than for larger firms. Moreover, SOX's disproportionate impact on these firms is entirely unwarranted, since the corporate meltdowns that led to it were a phenomenon of large corporations. To the extent that SOX addresses the problems in the latter, its provisions are not necessarily appropriate for small firms. In particular, small firms may have far less need for extensive internal controls provisions throughout the organization. Of course there will be a question as to what the dividing line should be for any "small firm" exemption. As with the provision suggested earlier in this chapter, this might be left to SEC rule.

As with foreign firms, Congress might give small firms the ability to opt into or out of SOX provisions. Small firms might be given this option only for certain provisions that are much more costly or less appropriate for them, such as the internal controls provision. Congress might also provide for a sliding scale in which the act or some of its provisions do not apply at all to the smallest firms, and allow opt-ins and opt-outs for medium-sized firms. This discussion indicates only some of the many alternatives to one-size-fits-all mandatory regulation Congress can pursue.

There is, of course, a question concerning the appropriate cutoff for smaller firms. The SEC's Advisory Committee on Smaller Public Companies has already done significant work on this issue. It has in process a general opt-in proposal that would specifically include the internal controls provision permitting opt-in for the smallest firms, defined as the smallest 1 percent by total capitalization and less than $125 million in annual revenue, and the next smallest 5 percent by total capitalization with less than $10 million in revenue. The committee's careful proposals reflect consideration of not only the differential reporting burdens and benefits of smaller firms, but also the need for standards that are transparent and relatively easy to apply.

It is important, however, to keep in mind that the Advisory Committee was constrained to operate within the existing statutory framework. Congress's mandate in revising the act, and the scope of any SEC rulemaking power under a revised act, might be significantly broader than what is permitted under current law. Moreover, any proposal to exempt small firms inherently creates a risk of giving firms perverse incentives to limit growth in order to avoid SOX's onerous requirements. Accordingly, the Advisory Committee's proposals cannot solve the problems SOX creates.

Remove Criminal Penalties

As discussed in chapter 4, SOX exacerbates the increasing over-criminalization of corporate law not only by increasing criminal penalties for violation of the securities laws, but by providing new crimes, particularly including those based on certification of inadequate internal controls. The dramatic post-Enron trials and plea bargains demonstrate not only the many powerful pre-SOX criminal sanctions that prosecutors have at their disposal, but also the potential for prosecutorial abuse of these sanctions. These sanctions make the corporate suite a very dangerous place even for law-abiding executives. They may react by avoiding public firms that are subject to SOX, or engaging in conduct that is far more conservative than diversified shareholders would prefer—including excessive attention to internal controls disclosures.

Criminal liability under SOX was one of the clearest examples of Congress's attempting to appease popular sentiment and engaging in symbolic politics rather than careful lawmaking.[14] But the firms and executives who must live under this regime, and the corporate criminal defendants, are not mere "symbols." If Congress has an opportunity to revisit SOX in a calmer atmosphere, one of its first responses should be to eliminate criminal liability under its provisions. To be sure, this would be only a partial response to the general problem of over-criminalization. But it could be an important first step.

Limit Internal Controls Reporting

SOX section 404 goes much too far in penalizing and even criminalizing executives' failure to spot not just problems, but even risks that later happen to turn into problems. If Congress concludes that it must retain section 404, it can at least revise the provision so that it does not impose the huge costs discussed in chapters 4–6. The revised law should clarify that managers can exercise reasonable business judgment about risks to report, and that these risks will be assessed as of the time the report is completed rather than in light of subsequent events.

Leave Internal Governance to State Law

Several SOX provisions amount to a federal takeover of the internal governance of corporations, which has traditionally, and rightly, been the province of state law. These include rules mandating audit committee independence, prohibiting certain executive loans, mandating forfeiture of executive compensation when earnings are later restated, and requiring lawyer reporting of corporate wrongdoing. Congress should consider repealing these provisions and returning these matters to state law, where they belong.

8

The Future: Regulatory Hubris or Greater Humility?

So far, we have shown the high costs and dubious benefits of SOX, as well as the powerful political forces that push for SOX and other corporate reforms. These problems do not represent a one-time regulatory quirk, but rather are inherent in corporate governance regulation. The forces that produced SOX have converged before and can be expected to converge again. The lesson from this discussion is that policy analysts and corporate law scholars need to be prepared for them.

Failure to be prepared can result in much more intrusive regulation with the next generation of "reform." As bad as SOX has been in many respects, it clearly could have gone further. SOX relies mostly on disclosure provisions that can have significant substantive governance implications. Its most invasive provisions, such as the executive loan prohibition, relate only to specific pockets of activities rather than spreading across the range of corporate decision-making.

What might be next? In a recent paper, James Fanto serves up a sobering vision of the future of the largest business firms being saddled with "monitors" employed by the SEC, who keep a close eye on the firm's management.[1] Fanto bases his suggestion on the regulations that already govern banks. This sort of invasive regulation is obviously inappropriate for entrepreneurial business corporations that are not subject to federal deposit insurance. The risk of failure and even fraud is built into any successful capitalist system, and can be shouldered by investors holding diversified portfolios of shares priced by efficient markets to reflect risk. But while the proposal flops as normative prescription, it might be worth a look as prediction. As long as our political leaders accept the idea that the law should strive to eliminate all risk of fraud to the extent possible—even at excessive cost—we should brace for the next set of reforms when the current ones fail at their impossible task.

It is entirely possible that the next boom and bust will bring the next regulatory panic, and with it another demand that Congress "restore confidence" in the market. The reformers will again step up, forgetting that SOX was supposed to be the law that ends all laws, ignoring the futility of trying to regulate away fraud, and urging yet another try. This time they will have Fanto's, or some similar proposal, queued up and ready to go.

Will the business community put up a united front against further encroachment, as it did not do against SOX? Not necessarily, because, as Fanto points out, it may be better for executives to accept a monitor who tells them what to do every step of the way than to accept the risk of liability when they do not follow the increasingly extensive rules. Fanto says:

> The business community may even find that it is in its interest not to oppose the corporate monitor, if it only recognizes that the regulation of public firm management is already a long way down the paternalistic road, but, at least with regards to enforcement, in a way that is not favorable to this management. Executives and board members are now sanctioned harshly for their faults by the SEC and federal prosecutors without having the kind of relationship with a regulator that might make unnecessary the sting of enforcement.

So the business community may be willing, next time, to accept a long-term "relationship" with regulators, rather than just the casual dating that occurs now.

There is a possible alternative to this dismal scenario. We can try to understand the true costs and benefits of regulation, and regulate in light of that understanding. This would involve regulators appreciating the significant limitations on government's ability both to eliminate fraud and to anticipate the full consequences of regulation. The following presents some suggestions of what regulating in light of this understanding might look like.

Periodic Review and Sunset Provisions

We have articulated the consequences and costs of SOX that Congress undoubtedly did not expect. These costs may become evident only after the effects of such an act are carefully tested. Important new legislation like SOX provides a sort of laboratory for financial economists. Although some of SOX's consequences and costs should have come as no surprise to dispassionate academic observers, chapter 1 demonstrates that Congress does not act in anything like the relaxed conditions of the ivory tower. Moreover, any legislation poses the risk of costs that no one can anticipate, including that business developments will render legal controls unnecessary.

For these reasons, significant new financial and governance regulation like SOX that displaces and supplements prior regulatory approaches should be subject to periodic review and sunset provisions. Although Congress, of course, can always undertake such reviews, prior experience indicates that it will not. Legislation is a one-way regulatory ratchet. It arises when the conditions for reform are ripe for a regulatory panic. The conditions for a "deregulatory panic" are less likely to develop. Firms learn to live with the extra costs and may not be willing or able to bear the costs of lobbying for repeal, at least in the absence of a regulatory cataclysm. Thus, it is not surprising that SOX sponsor Michael Oxley, despite recognizing that SOX was "excessive" in some respects, and admitting that it had been rushed through Congress, suggested that Congress would not be revisiting the issue, even as to the seriously affected small companies. He said, "If I had another crack at it I would have provided a bit more flexibility for small- and medium-sized companies."[2] In other words, Congress normally does not have "another crack" at regulation. A sunset or review mechanism would change that.

Perhaps Congress can learn some lessons from itself. The USA Patriot Act was passed less than one year before SOX and, like SOX, was passed by an overwhelming majority. Unlike SOX, the USA Patriot Act includes sunset provisions for some of its most controversial provisions.[3]

The Patriot Act's sunset provision forced Congress and the president to reevaluate and debate those provisions, in an atmosphere far removed from the immediate post-9/11 panic. American investors would benefit from a sober reevaluation of SOX. Perhaps the courts will provide that opportunity. For future regulatory panics, Congress would do well to remember the lessons of the Patriot Act.

Certification and Opt-Out Approaches

The law might regulate "humbly" by imposing optional rather than mandatory rules. For example, it could supplement market or private fraud-prevention mechanisms by prescribing a certification regime, and let firms decide whether they want to certify.[4] The government function here would be to provide an organization that could provide a signal of honesty that investors could rely on. But firms can decide for themselves whether the signal costs too much to send. Similarly, the government could prescribe a regulatory scheme but permit firms to opt out as long as they get the requisite approval from their owners and make the appropriate disclosures to investors.[5] For example, the law might, as in the United Kingdom, let firms "comply or explain"—that is, opt out of compliance as long as they explain that they are doing so and why.[6]

Nuanced Regulation

Regulation should take account of differences among firms and regulatory contexts. The best way to do that is to make the regulation optional. If mandatory rules are deemed necessary to fix significant market defects, Congress should focus them on the specific problems that cannot be dealt with by optional rules. It should also design the rules taking into account differences among firms as to the need for regulation and the costs of compliance. For example, Congress clearly should have scaled costs by firm size, as well as take into account the different internal governance structure of foreign firms subject to SOX.[7]

Investor Education

The corporate frauds addressed by SOX happened in part because of investors' willingness to ignore indications of questionable accounting and to accept extravagant claims about unproven business plans. These problems might be mitigated more cost-effectively by providing some minimal training in the basics of finance.[8] This education might help offset some judgment biases of investors, teach the rudiments of efficient markets and how hard it is for ordinary investors to "outsmart" the market, and warn them of the folly of not investing in diversified portfolios or index funds. Even if investors continue to fall for scams, at least they could be persuaded not to bet their life savings and retirements. For example, instead of trying to rid the market of all potential conflicts, including those that have net benefits for investors and firms, investors might be alerted to the problems of conflicts and then allowed to make their own judgments.[9]

Congress and the SEC could start this education process by ensuring that their own regulatory efforts do not mislead investors into believing that markets are safer than they are.[10] For example, moves toward subsidizing securities research for ordinary investors imply that they should be researching and investing in individual stocks. Shareholders are better off diversified and rationally ignorant.

Deregulation

Some problems in the securities markets could be mitigated by reducing the amount of regulation that already exists. An example is the SEC's regulation of disclosure to securities analysts. Analysts have strong incentives to ferret out information about firms, including information about potential fraud. Congress recognized the importance of their monitoring role by adding provisions to SOX concerning analyst conflicts.

Yet, prior to Enron, the SEC promulgated regulation FD, which had the effect of hobbling analysts' ability to get information. Regulation FD requires firms that disclose information privately to analysts also to make the information public.[11] This reduces analysts' incentives and ability to research by denying them the ability to have one-on-one conversations with corporate executives. It also reduces firms' incentives to disclose, since there is some information they need not make public, and they would rather not do so. For example, some pieces of information disclosed to trusted analysts might be subject to misinterpretation if released piecemeal to the market.[12] There is evidence that, in fact, some firms have chosen to stop disclosing information rather than disclose publicly.[13] Indeed, regulation FD may have given insiders an excuse to hide from inquiring analysts, where before they would trigger negative inferences by doing so. Thirty years ago, insurance industry analyst Ray Dirks broke the notorious Equity Funding scandal. Regulation FD may have inhibited him from performing a similar function today. Not surprisingly, there is evidence that analysts' forecasts have declined following regulation FD.[14]

Regulation FD is part of the SEC's and former chairman Arthur Levitt's quixotic quest to ensure "fairness" in information. This effort is doomed to failure because inequality of information is a basic fact of the securities markets. If one group is denied the information, another will get it.[15] The main effect of forced sharing of information is not to eliminate inequality but to weaken the incentives to gather and create information on which efficient securities markets rely. Although regulation FD may reduce firms' ability to "buy" analysts' support with exclusive information, it is far from clear that this is a serious problem, given the market's ability to punish biased analysts.

Conclusion

SOX was suspect from the beginning—enacted in haste in the middle of a regulatory panic with almost no deliberation on even its most important provisions, and little or no credible evidence supporting the need for new regulation of any kind.

Laws were already in place to deal with the fraudulent conduct that emerged with the bursting of the millennial bubble. It makes no sense to impose significant new regulation, even if this regulation might reduce fraud, if the costs of it exceed any possible benefit from fraud reduction. In fact, SOX has been horrendously costly, with the best evidence of its effect on market prices standing at almost a trillion and a half dollars.

Some of the costs of SOX are in the form of direct compliance, including the notorious internal controls provision and the burden of finding directors to comply with the new audit committee independence rules. SOX's defenders attempt to fall back on the argument that these direct costs (although much higher than even they expected them to be) will decline in time as firms put compliance systems in place. But even if this is the case, it is only a feeble response to SOX's problems, since we estimate that these direct compliance costs are only about a fifth of the total costs the act imposes.

SOX's indirect costs—both those that have already manifested, and those looming on the horizon—are legion. They include

- the costs of managing in the "climate of fear" created by SOX's myriad new liabilities and rules, particularly section 404, including constraints on managerial risk-taking;

- limits on executive compensation through the insider-loan prohibition;

- the opportunity costs of diverting executives' time from business management to paper management;

- the high costs imposed on small firms, effectively forcing many to forgo public ownership and reducing valuable entrepreneurial activity;

- the reduction in the flow of information and trust in firms by, among other things, turning employees and lawyers into hall monitors;

- the placing of the cost of business failure on corporate executives, thereby undoing the efficient diversification of risk enabled by public securities markets;

- a furthering of the trend toward criminalizing ordinary agency costs, with significant impact both on corporate management and the criminal justice system;

- the placing of significant new burdens and risks on auditors, thereby forcing additional inefficient risk-bearing that makes it even harder for smaller and riskier firms to enter the public markets;

- regulation of securities analysts that reduces their incentives to gather information important to market efficiency;

- interference with state regulation of corporate governance, which has been a significant reason for the success of our capital markets;

- the discouragement of foreign firms from trading in the United States, thereby eroding the U.S. dominance in world securities markets;

- the setting of a litigation time bomb that will explode in the next economic downturn, exposing firms to ruinous litigation from hindsight evaluation of their disclosures in response to SOX's new requirements.

SOX's defenders might persist even in the face of this litany of costs by saying that, despite the huge costs, our capital markets derive incalculable benefits from reducing the fraud that had eroded investor confidence prior to the passage of the act. However, even if we assume for the sake of argument that the risk of fraud is lower now than it was before SOX, it is not clear that this is a result of SOX's provisions or that the market or the states would not have responded on their own if SOX had not been adopted.

Congress should, and may have an opportunity and incentive to, reexamine SOX. Even if the result is not complete repeal, Congress should consider revisions that would reduce the horrendous costs SOX imposes. Possibilities include exempting foreign and small firms, eliminating criminal and civil penalties for violation of SOX, and permitting opt-in or opt-out of at least some of the act's provisions by at least some types of firms.

An understanding of these high costs and minimal benefits, and of the forces that produced this misguided legislation, may help to prevent a regulatory debacle in the future. We make specific recommendations for any future regulation of the capital markets that are suggested by the SOX experience, including optional provisions, periodic review and sunset provisions, and regulation whose scope is more carefully designed and focused. SOX should teach us to respond to fraud in a more measured way, with regulation that works with, rather than against, markets.

Notes

Introduction

1. Adolf Berle and Gardiner Means, *The Modern Corporation and Private Property* (New York: Macmillan, 1932).

2. "Learning to Love Sarbanes-Oxley," *Business Week*, November 21, 2005, http://www.businessweek.com/magazine/content/05_47/b3960113 .htm (accessed April 10, 2006); Joe Nocera, "For All Its Cost, Sarbanes Law is Working," *New York Times*, December 3, 2005, http://select.nytimes .com/search/restricted/article?res=F00A1EFA39550C708CDDAB0994DD4 04482 (accessed April 3, 2006); James Surowiecki, "SOXed-In?" *New Yorker*, December 12, 2005, http://www.newyorker.com/talk/content/ articles/051212ta_talk_surowiecki (accessed April 3, 2006). For a response to all of these articles, see William Sjostrom, *Ideoblog*, http://busmovie. typepad.com/ideoblog/2005/12/another_prosox_.html (accessed April 3, 2006). For responses to the Nocera article, see Stephen Bainbridge, "Shedding Light on SOX," December 7, 2005, http://www.tcsdaily.com/ article.aspx?id=120705G (accessed April 3, 2006). For responses to the *Business Week* article, see Dale Oesterle, "Business Law Professors Square Off over Sarbanes-Oxley," *Business Law Prof Blog*, December 3, 2005 http://lawprofessors.typepad.com/business_law/2005/12/business_law_ pr.html (accessed April 3, 2006), and William Sjostrom, "A Silver Lining in Sarbanes-Oxley," *Business Law Prof Blog*, November 14, 2005, http:// lawprofessors.typepad.com/business_law/2005/11/silver_lining_i.html (accessed April 3, 2006).

3. See Nocera, "For All Its Cost."

4. The assertion that Congress should be in the management consulting business is laughable and brings to mind President Ronald Reagan's famous quote: "The ten most feared words in the English language are 'Hi, I'm from the government and I'm here to help.'"

5. Michael G. Oxley, "In the Wake of the Sarbanes-Oxley Act," *Ohio Northern University Law Review* 31 no. 3 (2005): 319–24.

6. Arthur Levitt Jr., "A Misguided Exemption," *Wall Street Journal*, A8, January 27, 2006, http://online.wsj.com/article/SB113833559392957970.html?mod=todays_us_opinion%20 (accessed April 3, 2006). As to the role of Levitt and other "policy entrepreneurs" in obtaining passage of SOX, see chapter 1. Also, see pp. 91–92 for more on the proposed exemptions.

7. The different positions of the big and small business lobbies on SOX are discussed below in chapter 1.

8. See AMR Research, "SOX Spending for 2006 To Exceed $6B," November 29, 2005, http://www.amrresearch.com/Content/View.asp?pmillid=18967 (accessed April 3, 2006).

9. Assuming that the $6 billion will continue as an annual payment in perpetuity, and assuming an interest rate of 2 percent, the present discounted value of the direct costs is "only" $300 billion.

10. The complaint may be found at http://www.feinstitute.org/pdfs/FEF%20v%20%20PCAOB%20Complaint.pdf (accessed April 3, 2006). For a discussion of the suit, see "A Matter of Oversight," *Economist* (U.S.), February 18, 2006, 71. For analysis of this issue, see Donna M. Nagy, "Playing Peekaboo With Constitutional Law: The PCAOB and its Public/Private Status," *Notre Dame Law Review* 80, no. 3 (March 2005): 975–1072, available at http://ssrn.com/abstract=622964 (accessed April 3, 2006).

Chapter 1: From Enron to SOX

1. See Samuel E. Bodily and Robert F. Bruner, "Enron, 1986–2001," Social Science Research Network Case and Teaching Paper Series, Darden Case No. UVA-G-0563-M-SSRN, 2002, http://papers.ssrn.com/sol3/papers.cfm?abstract_id=302155 (accessed March 21, 2006).

2. William C. Powers, Jr. et al., Report of Investigation By the Special Investigative Committee of The Board of Directors of Enron Corp., February 1, 2002, http://files.findlaw.com/news.findlaw.com/wp/docs/enron/specinv020102rpt1.pdf (accessed March 29, 2006).

3. See Roberta Romano, "The Sarbanes-Oxley Act and the Making of Quack Corporate Governance," *Yale Law Journal* 114, no. 7 (May 2005): 1521–1611. See also Jayne W. Barnard, "Historical Quirks, Political Opportunism, and the Anti-Loan Provision of the Sarbanes-Oxley Act," *Ohio Northern University Law Review* 31, no. 3 (2005): 325–58 (also presenting detailed legislative history and background, focusing on executive loan provisions).

4. *Wikipedia*, s.v. "Sarbanes-Oxley Act," http://en.wikipedia.org/wiki/Sarbanes-Oxley_Act (accessed March 29, 2006).

5. For a skeptical analysis of the alleged lack of "investor confidence" leading up to the enactment of SOX, see Peter J. Wallison, "Sarbanes-Oxley as an Inside-the-Beltway Phenomenon," AEI Online, June 1, 2004, http://www.aei.org/publications/filter.all,pubID.20582/pub_detail.asp (accessed April 3, 2006).

6. See chapter 6, below.

7. Romano, "The Sarbanes-Oxley Act and the Making of Quack Corporate Governance," 1559; Karlyn H. Bowman, "Sarbanes-Oxley and Public Opinion After Enron and WorldCom," paper presented at the American Enterprise Institute event, "Sarbanes-Oxley: A Review," May 5, 2004, http://www.aei.org/events/eventID.809,filter.all/event_detail.asp (accessed April 3, 2006). Follow "video" link, at 00:13:45, for discussion of data compiled by the Media Research Center.

8. David P. Baron, "Persistent Media Bias," Social Science Research Network Working Paper Series, Research Paper No. 1845, Stanford Graduate School of Business, 2004, http://ssrn.com/abstract=516006 (accessed March 21, 2006).

9. Michael C. Jensen, "Toward a Theory of the Press," in *Economics and Social Institutions*, ed. Karl Brunner (The Hague: Martinus Nijhoff Publishing Company, 1979).

10. John E. Core, Wayne R. Guay, and David F. Larcker, "The Power of the Pen and Executive Compensation," Social Science Research Network Working Paper Series, October 28, 2005, http://ssrn.com/abstract=838347 (accessed March 10, 2006).

11. See, generally, Mancur Olson, *The Logic of Collective Action* (Cambridge, Mass.: Harvard University Press, 1965); Robert E. McCormick and Robert D. Tollison, *Politicians, Legislation, and the Economy: An Inquiry into the Interest Group Theory of Government* (Boston: Kluwer, 1981); Robert Tollison, "Public Choice and Legislation," *Virginia Law Review* 74, no. 2 (March 1988): 339–72.

12. See Romano, "The Sarbanes-Oxley Act and the Making of Quack Corporate Governance."

13. See Henry G. Manne, "Economic Aspects of Required Disclosure under Federal Securities Law," in *Wall Street in Transition: The Emerging System and its Impact on the Economy*, ed. Henry G. Manne and Ezra Solomon (New York: New York University Press, 1974), 33–36.

14. See Richard B. Schmitt, "Lawyers' Growth Industry: Corporate Probes," *Wall Street Journal*, June 28, 2002, B1 (discussing how lawyers specializing in internal corporate investigations are profiting by recent corporate fraud scandals).

15. Nocera, "For All Its Cost."

16. The accounting profession, in other words, was "born and bred in the briar patch." See Joel Chandler Harris, "Brer Rabbit and the Tar Baby," http://www.otmfan.com/html/brertar.htm (accessed March 10, 2006).

17. Jonathan R. Macey, "The Politicalization of American Corporate Governance," Conference on Boundaries of SEC Regulation, Claremont McKenna Financial Economics Institute, February 3, 2006.

18. See Romano, "The Sarbanes-Oxley Act and the Making of Quack Corporate Governance," 1586–87.

19. Elisabeth Bumiller, "Bush Faces Scrutiny over Disclosing '90 Stock Sale Late," New York Times, July 4, 2002, A11. For a discussion of how Bush's political problems related specifically to the adoption of the executive loan provisions in SOX, see Barnard, "Historical Quirks."

20. See Romano, "The Sarbanes-Oxley Act and the Making of Quack Corporate Governance," 1562.

21. Joann S. Lublin, "Loans to Corporate Officers Unlikely to Cease Soon," Wall Street Journal, July 10, 2002, A8.

22. See Barnard, "Historical Quirks," 338.

23. Ibid., 340.

24. George Miller (U.S. Representative, R-Cal.), quoted in Carolyn Lochhead, "Bush to Sign Corporate Crackdown: GOP Drops Opposition, Backs Tougher Version," San Francisco Chronicle, July 25, 2002, A1.

25. See Romano, "The Sarbanes-Oxley Act and the Making of Quack Corporate Governance," 1568–85.

26. See ibid., 1534n35, and Zoe-Vonna Palmrose and Ralph S. Saul, "The Push for Auditor Independence," Regulation, Winter 2001, 20, http://www.cato.org/pubs/regulation/regv24n4/v24n4-3.pdf (accessed March 10, 2006).

27. Romano, "The Sarbanes-Oxley Act and the Making of Quack Corporate Governance," 1583.

28. See ibid., 1555–58.

29. See American Bar Association, "Report of the American Bar Association Task Force on Corporate Responsibility," March 31, 2003, http://www.abanet.org/buslaw/corporateresponsibility/final_report.pdf (accessed March 10, 2006).

30. Romano, "The Sarbanes-Oxley Act and the Making of Quack Corporate Governance," 1585–91.

31. See Barnard, "Historical Quirks," 338–39.

32. Joann S. Lublin, "Questioning the Books: The President Speaks: Loans to Corporate Officers Unlikely to Cease Soon," Wall Street Journal, July 10, 2002, A8.

33. Barnard, "Historical Quirks," 339n102.

34. Sarbanes-Oxley Act of 2002, S6690, 107th Cong., 2d sess. *Congressional Record* 148 (daily ed. July 12, 2002), quoted in Barnard, "Historical Quirks," 339.

35. Ibid.

36. See Larry E. Ribstein, "Sarbox: The Road to Nirvana," *Michigan State Law Review* 2004, no. 2 (2004): 279–98.

37. See Ribstein, "Bubble Laws," *Houston Law Review* 40 (Spring 2003), 77–97. See also Stuart Banner, "What Causes New Securities Regulation? 300 Years of Evidence," *Washington University Law Quarterly* 75, no. 2 (Summer 1997): 850 (showing that securities market regulation in the United Kingdom and the United States in the eighteenth and nineteenth centuries was adopted only after stock market declines); Romano, "The Sarbanes-Oxley Act and the Making of Quack Corporate Governance," 1591–94 (discussing regulation as a function of stock market declines).

38. Romano, "The Sarbanes-Oxley Act and the Making of Quack Corporate Governance," 1551–68.

Chapter 2: What Shareholders Want— The Optimal Amount of Fraud

1. Berle and Means, *Modern Corporation and Private Property*.

2. Market forces provide strong incentives for contracting parties to perform as promised. In this view, corporate law plays the important role of providing standard terms and gap-fillers that define the legal relationships among the parties. See Frank H. Easterbrook and Daniel R. Fischel, *The Economic Structure of Corporate Law* (Cambridge, Mass.: Harvard University Press, 1991), 1–39, and Henry N. Butler, "The Contractual Theory of the Corporation," *George Mason Law Review* 11, no. 4 (Summer 1989): 99–124. The contractarian approach to corporate law suggests that corporations should be free to alter the default rules. See Henry N. Butler and Larry E. Ribstein, "Opting Out of Fiduciary Duties: A Response to the Anti-Contractarians," *Washington Law Review* 65, no. 1 (January 1990): 71, and Frank H. Easterbrook and Daniel R. Fischel, "Contract and Fiduciary Duty," *Journal of Law and Economics* 36, no. 1–2 (1993): 425–51.

3. For an analysis of the rationales for and functions of the business judgment rule, see Larry E. Ribstein, "Accountability and Responsibility in Corporate Governance," *Notre Dame Law Review* 81, no. 4 (2006, forthcoming).

Chapter 3: Imagining a World Without SOX

1. See Nocera, "For All Its Cost, Sarbanes Law is Working."

2. See Oxley, "In the Wake of the Sarbanes-Oxley Act," 320–21.

3. For evidence that there was no lack of investor confidence, see Wallison, "Sarbanes-Oxley As An Inside-the-Beltway Phenomenon," 15.

4. See William H. Beaver, "What Have We Learned from the Recent Corporate Scandals that We Did Not Already Know?" *Stanford Journal of Law, Business and Finance* 8, no. 1 (Autumn 2002): 155–68.

5. See Richard M. Frankel, Marilyn F. Johnson, and Karen K. Nelson, "The Relation Between Auditors' Fees for Non-Audit Services and Earnings Quality," Social Science Research Network Working Paper Series, Working Paper No. 4330-02, MIT Sloan, January 2002, http://papers.ssrn.com/paper .taf?abstract_id=296557 (accessed March 21, 2006).

6. Jonathan Karpoff, D. Scott Lee, and Gerald S. Martin, "The Cost to Firms of Cooking the Books," Social Science Research Network Working Paper Series, July 25, 2005, http://papers.ssrn.com/paper.taf?abstract_ id=652121 (accessed March 21, 2006).

7. Hemang Desai, Chris E. Hogan, and Michael Wilkins, "The Reputational Penalty for Aggressive Accounting: Earnings Restatements and Management Turnover," *Accounting Review* 81, no. 1 (January 2006): 83–112.

8. See Jonathan R. Laing, "The Bear that Roared: How Short-Seller Jim Chanos Helped Expose Enron," *Wall Street Journal Online*, January 28, 2002, http://online.wsj.com/barrons/article/0,4298,SB101191069416063240 .djm,00.html (accessed March 10, 2006).

9. William W. Bratton, "Enron and the Dark Side of Shareholder Value," *Tulane Law Review* 76, no. 5–6 (June 2002): 1275–1362.

10. See George A. Akerlof, "The Market for 'Lemons': Quality Uncertainty and the Market Mechanism," *Quarterly Journal of Economics* 84, no. 3 (1970): 488–500.

11. See, for example, A. Michael Spence, *Market Signaling: Informational Transfer in Hiring and Related Processes* (Cambridge, Mass.: Harvard University Press, 1974).

12. Benjamin Klein and Keith B. Leffler, "The Role of Market Forces in Assuring Contractual Performance," *Journal of Political Economy* 89, no. 4 (1981): 615–41; Oliver Williamson, "Credible Commitments: Using Hostages to Support Exchange," *American Economic Review* 73, no. 4 (September 1983): 519–40.

13. See Stephen J. Choi and Marcel Kahan, "The Market Penalty for Mutual Fund Scandals," Social Science Research Network Working Paper Series, Law and Economics Research Paper No. 06-07, New York University, January 2006, http://papers.ssrn.com/sol3/papers.cfm?abstract_id=877896 (accessed March 21, 2006).

14. See John E. Core, "The Directors' and Officers' Insurance Premium: An Outside Assessment of the Quality of Corporate Governance," *Journal of Law Economics, and Organization* 16, no. 2 (October 2000): 449–77 (showing a significant association between directors' and officers' premiums and proxies for the quality of firms' governance structures, which is confirmed by positive correlation between firms' insurance premiums and excessive CEO compensation).

15. See Joshua Ronen, "Post-Enron Reform: Financial Statement Insurance, and Gaap Re-Visited," *Stanford Journal of Law, Business and Finance* 8, no. 1 (Autumn 2002): 39–68.

16. See SEC Rule 14a-8.

17. See Roberta Romano, *The Genius of American Corporate Law* (Washington, D.C.: AEI Press, 1993).

18. William Cary, "Federalism and Corporate Law: Reflections Upon Delaware," *Yale Law Journal* 83, no. 4 (March 1974): 663–705; Ralph Winter, "State Law, Shareholder Protection, and the Theory of the Corporation," *Journal of Legal Studies* 6, no. 2 (June 1977): 251–92. For more recent versions of Cary's view, see Lucian Arye Bebchuk and Allen Ferrell, "Federalism and Takeover Law: The Race to Protect Managers from Takeovers," *Columbia Law Review* 99, no. 5 (June 1999): 1168–99, and Lucian Arye Bebchuk, "Federalism and the Corporation: The Desirable Limits on State Competition in Corporate Law," *Harvard Law Review* 105, no. 7 (May 1992): 1435–1510.

19. See Sanjai Bhagat and Roberta Romano, "Event Studies and the Law: Part II: Empirical Studies of Corporate Law," *American Law and Economics Review* 4, no. 2 (Fall 2002): 382–94 (reviewing studies relating to state competition debate); Peter Dodd and Richard Leftwich, "The Market for Corporate Charters: 'Unhealthy Competition' versus Federal Regulation," *Journal of Business* 53, no. 3 (1980): 259–83 (showing "management's decision to reincorporate in another state does not reduce stockholder wealth"); Roberta Romano, "The Need for Competition in International Securities Regulation," *Theoretical Inquiries in Law* 2, no. 2 (July 2001): 495–97 (reviewing eight studies finding positive abnormal stock returns from changing incorporation state).

20. See William B. Chandler III and Leo E. Strine Jr., "The New Federalism of the American Corporate Governance System: Preliminary Reflections of

Two Residents of One Small State," *University of Pennsylvania Law Review* 152, no. 2 (December 2003): 953–1006.

21. Enron reincorporated from Delaware to Oregon in 1997 in order to buy an Oregon electric utility, Portland General Electric, and be eligible for the intrastate exemption of the Public Utility Holding Company Act. See Senate Committee on Governmental Affairs, *Financial Oversight of Enron: The SEC and Private-Sector Watchdogs*, 107th Cong., 2d sess., 26, October 8, 2002, 2002 WL 31267528. Georgia led the country in adoption of a particularly effective "dead-hand" poison pill. See *Invacare Corp. v. Healthdyne Tech. Inc.*, 968 F. Supp. 1578 (N.D. Ga. 1997), a device Delaware invalidated in *Quickturn Design Sys. v. Mentor Graphics Corp.*, 721 A.2d 1281 (Del. 1998); *Carmody v. Toll Bros. Inc.*, 723 A.2d 1180 (Del. Ch. 1998).

22. Delaware courts are well-suited to responding quickly to the regulatory challenge presented by corporate fraud. See Jill E. Fisch, "The Peculiar Role of the Delaware Courts in the Competition for Corporate Charters," *University of Cincinnati Law Review* 68, no. 4 (Summer 2000): 1061–1100.

23. Mark J. Roe, "Delaware's Competition," *Harvard Law Review* 117, no. 2 (December 2003): 588–646.

24. See Sanjai Bhagat and Bernard Black, "The Non-Correlation Between Board Independence and Long-Term Firm Performance," *Journal of Corporation Law* 27, no. 2 (Winter 2002): 231–74; Sanjai Bhagat and Bernard Black, "The Uncertain Relationship Between Board Composition and Firm Performance," *Business Lawyer* 54, no. 3 (May 1999): 921–64; Bhagat and Romano, "Event Studies and the Law," 402–3.

25. See Barnard, "Historical Quirks."

26. See Stephen J. Choi and Andrew T. Guzman, "Portable Reciprocity: Rethinking the International Reach of Securities Regulation," *Southern California Law Review* 71, no. 5 (July 1998): 903–52; Roberta Romano, "Empowering Investors: A Market Approach to Securities Regulation," *Yale Law Journal* 107, no. 8 (June 1998): 2359–2430. For criticisms of these proposals, see James D. Cox, "Regulatory Duopoly in U.S. Securities Markets," *Columbia Law Review* 99, no. 5 (June 1999): 1200–52; Merritt Fox, "Securities Disclosure in a Globalizing Market: Who Should Regulate Whom," *Michigan Law Review* 95, no. 8 (August 1997): 2498–2632.

27. See Larry E. Ribstein, "Cross-Listing and Regulatory Competition," *Review of Law and Economics* 1, no. 1, article 7 (2005), http://www.bepress.com/rle/vol1/iss1/art7 (accessed March 11, 2006).

28. See, generally, Paul G. Mahoney, "The Exchange as Regulator," *Virginia Law Review* 83, no. 7 (October 1997): 1453–1500.

29. See New York Stock Exchange, "Corporate Governance Rule Proposals Reflecting Recommendations from the NYSE Corporate Accountability and Listing Standards Committee as Approved by the NYSE Board of Directors," August 16, 2002, http://www.nyse.com/pdfs/corp_gov_pro_b.pdf (accessed April 3, 2006). Rules would require a majority of the board to have no material relationships with the firm and lengthen to five years the "cooling-off" period for board service by former employees of the issuer or its auditor; require that directors meet without management; require wholly independent nominating and compensation committees in addition to the independent audit committee; require the chair of the audit committee to have accounting or financial management expertise; require the audit committee to have sole responsibility for hiring the auditing firm; and prohibit compensation of audit committee members apart from directors' fees.

30. There is some reason to believe that stock exchanges no longer can fulfill the function of regulating the governance of listed firms. Jonathan Macey and Maureen O'Hara argue persuasively that changing technology has lowered the cost of trading, which has facilitated the emergence of competing trading venues, in turn affecting the viability of exchanges as regulators. Jonathan R. Macey and Maureen O'Hara, "From Markets to Venues: Securities Regulation in an Evolving World," *Stanford Law Review* 58, no. 2 (November 2005): 563–99. Among other problems, exchanges cannot effectively discipline listed firms that have a variety of trading venues. Also, with so many available trading venues, an exchange does not internalize the benefits of its regulatory efforts, and therefore has an incentive to invest too little in regulation and enforcement. As a result, "self-regulation" by the exchanges is really regulation forced, or at least strongly urged, by the SEC.

31. See Gilles Hilary and Clive Lennox, "The Credibility of Self-Regulation: Evidence from the Accounting Profession's Peer Review Program," *Journal of Accounting and Economics* 40, no. 1–3 (2005): 211–29 (showing that opinions issued by peer reviewers have provided credible information, based on evidence that audit firms gained clients after receiving clean opinions from their reviewers and lost clients after receiving modified or adverse opinions). Also see Paul V. Dunmore and Haim Falk, "Economic Competition between Professional Bodies: The Case of Auditing," *American Law and Economics Review* 3, no. 2 (2001): 302–19 (showing that competition among professional

auditing associations can efficiently substitute for most government regulation).

Chapter 4: The Costs of SOX

1. See Ivy Xiying Zhang, "Economic Consequences of the Sarbanes-Oxley Act of 2002," unpublished paper, 2005, http://w4.stern.nyu.edu/accounting/docs/speaker_papers/spring2005/Zhang_Ivy_Economic_Consequences_of_S_O.pdf (accessed March 11, 2006).

2. See Securities and Exchange Commission, "Certification of Disclosure in Companies' Quarterly and Annual Reports," Release 33-8124, August 29, 2002, http://www.sec.gov/rules/final/33-8124.htm (accessed April 3, 2006); Securities and Exchange Commission, "Final Rule: Management's Reports on Internal Control Over Financial Reporting and Certification of Disclosure in Exchange Act Periodic Reports," Release 33-8238, June 5, 2003, http://www.sec.gov/rules/final/33-8238.htm (accessed April 3, 2006).

3. See SEC Rules 13a–15(f), 15(d)–15(f).

4. See SEC Release 33-8238.

5. See SEC Rules 13a–15(c), 15d–15(c); SEC Release 33-8238.

6. See §103(a)(2)(A)(iii).

7. Securities and Exchange Commission, "Proposed Rule: Disclosure Required by Sections 404, 406 and 407 of the Sarbanes-Oxley Act of 2002," Release 33-8138, October 22, 2002, http://www.sec.gov/rules/proposed/33-8138.htm (accessed April 3, 2006).

8. See, e.g., Cary Klafter (director of corporate affairs, Legal Department, Intel Corporation), "Comment Letter," File No S7-40-02; Disclosure Required by Sections 404, 406, and 407 of the Sarbanes-Oxley Act of 2002, November 27, 2002 (stating that "based on our actual experience to date, we believe that the Commission has underestimated the time and effort involved in complying with these rules by at least a factor of 100, if not a greater order of magnitude") http://www.sec.gov/rules/proposed/s74002/cklafter1.txt (accessed April 3, 2006).

9. SEC Release 33-8238, n. 174.

10. Financial Executives International, "Sarbanes-Oxley Compliance Costs Exceed Estimates," http://www.fei.org/404_survey_3_21_05.cfm (accessed April 3, 2006); AMR Research, "SOX Spending for 2006 To Exceed $6B."

11. Securities and Exchange Commission, "Management's Report on Internal Control over Financial Reporting and Certification of Disclosure in Exchange Act Periodic Reports of Non-Accelerated Filers and Foreign Private Issuers," Release 33-8545, March 2, 2005 (extending compliance

date for nonaccelerated filers and foreign private issuers to fiscal years ending after July 15, 2006), http://www.sec.gov/rules/final/33-8545.htm (accessed April 3, 2006); Securities and Exchange Commission, "Management's Report on Internal Control over Financial Reporting and Certification of Disclosure in Exchange Act Periodic Reports of Companies that are not Accelerated Filers," Release 33-8618, September 22, 2005 (extending compliance date for nonaccelerated filers to July 15, 2007), http://www.sec.gov/rules/final/33-8618.pdf (accessed April 7, 2006); SEC Advisory Committee on Smaller Public Companies, "Final Report of the Advisory Committee on Smaller Public Companies to the U.S. Securities and Exchange Commission," April 23, 2006, http://www.sec.gov/info/smallbus/acspc/acspc-finalreport.pdf (accessed April 25, 2006); Securities and Exchange Commission, "Staff Statement on Management's Report on Internal Control Over Financial Reporting," May 16, 2005 (results of the roundtable and a "guidance" issued by the SEC), http://www.sec.gov/info/accountants/stafficreporting.htm (accessed April 3, 2006); Securities and Exchange Commission, "Roundtable Discussion on Implementation of Internal Control Reporting Provisions," April 13, 2005 (transcript of the roundtable), http://www.sec.gov/spotlight/soxcomp/soxcomp-trans.txt (accessed April 3, 2006).

12. The policy statements are at www.sec.gov/news/press/2005-74.htm (accessed April 3, 2006) and http://www.pcaobus.org/Rules/Docket_008/2005-05-16_Release_2005-009.pdf (accessed April 3, 2006), respectively.

13. Cynthia Glassman, Remarks before the Conference on Listed Companies and Legislators in Dialogue, Danish Ministry of Economic and Business Affairs, Copenhagen, Denmark, November 17, 2005, http://www.sec.gov/news/speech/spch111705cag.htm. (accessed April 3, 2006).

14. As the SEC Advisory Committee has noted ("Final Report," 29), Auditing Standard No. 2 was developed for external auditors and "does not provide management with guidance on how to document and test internal control or how to evaluate deficiencies identified," despite the fact that SOX section 404 clearly provides for different requirements for managers and for external auditors.

15. See, for example, survey data compiled by CRA International, "Sarbanes-Oxley Section 404 Costs and Implementation Issues: Survey Update," December 8, 2005, http://www.crai.com/pubs/pub_4896.pdf (accessed April 3, 2006).

16. See SEC Advisory Committee, "Final Report," 29–30, discussing this history.

17. This is summarized in Larry E. Ribstein, "Market v. Regulatory Responses to Corporate Fraud," *Journal of Corporation Law* 28, no. 1 (Fall 2002): 26–29.

18. Romano, "The Sarbanes-Oxley Act and the Making of Quack Corporate Governance," 1532.

19. See James S. Linck, Jeffry M. Netter, and Tina Yang, "Effects and Unintended Consequences of the Sarbanes-Oxley Act on Corporate Boards," Social Science Research Network Working Paper Series, March 2005, http://papers.ssrn.com/paper.taf?abstract_id=687496 (accessed March 21, 2006).

20. For a discussion of the business effects of SOX compliance, see Brian Doherty, "You Can Be Too Careful," *Reason*, January 2006, http://www.reason.com/0601/fe.bd.you.shtml (accessed April 3, 2006).

21. SEC Release 33-8238, n. 79.

22. Daniel A. Cohen, Aiyesha Day, and Thomas Lys, "The Sarbanes Oxley Act of 2002: Implications for Compensation Structure and Risk-Taking Incentives of CEOs," Social Science Research Network Working Paper Series, July 23, 2004, http://papers.ssrn.com/paper.taf?abstract_id=568483 (accessed March 21, 2006).

23. Peter J. Wallison, "Blame Sarbanes-Oxley," AEI Online, September 1, 2003, http://www.aei.org/publications/filter.all,pubID.19123/pub_detail.asp (accessed April 3, 2006).

24. See I.R.C. §162(m).

25. Financial Economists Roundtable, statement on "The Controversy Over Executive Compensation," November 24, 2003, http://www.luc.edu/orgs/finroundtable/statement03.pdf (accessed April 3, 2006).

26. See Robert F. Göx, "Tax Incentives for Inefficient Executive Pay and Reward for Luck," Social Science Research Network Working Paper Series, October 2005, http://ssrn.com/abstract=823884 (accessed March 21, 2006).

27. See Lucian Bebchuk and Jesse Fried, *Pay Without Performance: The Unfulfilled Promise of Executive Compensation* (Cambridge, Mass.: Harvard University Press, 2004); Securities Exchange Commission, "Proposed Rule Change: Executive Compensation and Related Party Disclosure," Release 33-8655, January 27, 2005, http://sec.gov/rules/proposed/33-8655.pdf (accessed April 3, 2006).

28. See Ribstein, "Sarbox: The Road to Nirvana"; Charles M. Elson, "The Duty of Care, Compensation, and Stock Ownership," *University of Cincinnati Law Review* 63, no. 2 (Winter 1995): 695.

29. See Khuldeep Shastri and Kathleen M. Kahle, "Executive Loans," Social Science Research Network Working Paper Series, EFA 2003 Annual

Conference Paper No. 184, AFA 2004 San Diego meetings, February 2003, p. 10 (showing that insider loans from 1996–2000 made to facilitate stock purchases were often diverted to other uses), http://ssrn.com/abstract=423447 (accessed March 22, 2006); Elizabeth A. Gordon, Elaine Henry, and Darius Palia, "Related Party Transactions: Associations with Corporate Governance and Firm Value," Social Science Research Network Working Paper Series, EFA 2004 Maastricht Meetings Paper No. 4377, p. 6, August 2004 (finding a negative relationship between industry-adjusted returns and insider loans), http://ssrn.com/abstract=558983 (accessed March 22, 2006).

30. See Barnard, "Historical Quirks," 349.

31. See chapter 1.

32. See Barnard, "Historical Quirks," 350–51.

33. Deborah Solomon, "Sarbanes and Oxley Agree to Disagree," *Wall Street Journal*, July 24, 2003, C1.

34. The SEC eventually provided limited guidance as to the legitimacy of foreign bank loans to bank executives; Securities and Exchange Commission, "SEC Adopts Fund Disclosure Rules and Foreign Bank Loan Exemption; Proposes Shell Company Rules," http://www.sec.gov/news/press/2004-50.htm (accessed April 3, 2006). The Department of Labor eventually clarified the application to ERISA plans; Field Assistance Bulletin 2003-1, April 15, 2003, http://www.dol.gov/ebsa/regs/fab_2003-1.html (accessed April 3, 2006). See also Mayer, Brown, Rowe, and Maw, "Sarbanes-Oxley Act: Interpretive Issues Under §402—Prohibition of Certain Insider Loans," www.mayerbrown.com/sarbanesoxley/interpretiveissuesundersec402.pdf (accessed March 12, 2006), and Mark R. Patterson, "Law-Fixing: Should Lawyers Agree How to Interpret Statutes?" Social Science Research Network Working Paper Series, PUB-LAW Research Papers No. 50, Fordham School of Law, p. 18-9, May 5, 2004, http://ssrn.com/abstract=555706 (accessed March 21, 2006). For a counterargument and other observations, see Larry E. Ribstein, "Should Lawyers Agree How to Interpret Statutes?" Ideoblog, January 11, 2005, http://busmovie.typepad.com/ideoblog/2005/01/should_lawyers_.html (accessed April 3, 2006).

35. See SEC Advisory Committee, "Final Report," 96–97.

36. Jill E. Fisch and Caroline M. Gentile, "The Qualified Legal Compliance Committee: Using the Attorney Conduct Rules to Restructure the Board of Directors," *Duke Law Journal* 53, no. 2 (November 2003): 583.

37. Robert Eli Rosen, "Resistances to Reforming Corporate Governance: The Diffusion of QLCC's," *Fordham Law Review* 74, no. 3 (December 2005): 1251–1318,

available at http://papers.ssrn.com/paper.taf?abstract_id=830131 (accessed March 21, 2006).

38. See Larry E. Ribstein, "Limited Liability of Professional Firms after Enron," *Journal of Corporation Law* 29, no. 2 (Winter 2004): 427–48.

39. See Deborah Solomon, "For Financial Whistle-Blowers, New Shield is an Imperfect One," *Wall Street Journal*, October 4, 2004, A1.

40. See Milton Friedman, *There's No Such Thing as a Free Lunch* (LaSalle, Ill.: Open Court, 1975).

41. See Michael C. Jensen and Kevin J. Murphy, "Performance Pay and Top Management Incentives," in Michael C. Jensen, *Foundations of Organizational Strategy* (Cambridge, Mass.: Harvard University Press, 1998).

42. See *BusinessWeek Online*, "Going Private," February 27, 2006, http://www.businessweek.com/magazine/content/06_09/b3973001.htm (accessed April 3, 2006).

43. See William J. Carney, "The Costs of Being Public After Sarbanes-Oxley: The Irony of 'Going Private,'" Social Science Research Network Working Paper Series, Emory Law and Economics Research Paper No. 05-4, February 2005, http://papers.ssrn.com/paper.taf?abstract_id= 672761 (accessed March 21, 2006).

44. See Jeffrey T. Doyle, Weili Ge, and Sarah E. McVay, "Determinants of Weaknesses in Internal Control Over Financial Reporting," Social Science Research Network Working Paper Series, July 2005, http://papers.ssrn.com/paper.taf?abstract_id=770465 (accessed March 21, 2006).

45. See Jason Scott Johnston, "Signaling Social Responsibility: On the Law and Economics of Market Incentives for Corporate Environmental Performance," Social Science Research Network Working Paper Series, University of Pennsylvania, Institute for Law and Economics Research Paper 05-16, May 11, 2005, http://papers.ssrn.com/paper.taf?abstract_id=725103 (accessed March 21, 2006); Michael P. Vandenbergh, "The Private Life of Public Law: Accounting for the Influence of Private Agreements on Public Regulation," *Columbia Law Review* 105, no. 7 (November 2005): 2029–96.

46. See Ellen Engel, Rachel M. Hayes, and Xue Wang, "The Sarbanes-Oxley Act and Firms' Going-Private Decisions," Social Science Research Network Working Paper Series, 2004, http://papers.ssrn.com/sol3/papers.cfm?abstract_id=546626 (accessed March 21, 2006).

47. See ARC Morgan, "Using Reported Weakness Disclosures to Benchmark Internal Controls" (showing that companies with sales of less than $250 million incurred $1.56 million in costs on internal controls, while firms with sales of $1 billion– $2 billion incurred $2.4 million in costs, including internal costs, opportunity costs, and intangibles); and SEC Advisory Committee,

"Final Report," 32–37 (including graphs showing post-SOX external audit fees as percentage of revenue much higher for smaller companies, and higher ratios of audit fees to capitalization and compliance costs to revenues).

48. SEC Advisory Committee, "Final Report," p. 5, table 1 (showing that such firms represent about 78.5 percent of total companies by number, but only about 6 percent by capitalization), and 35–36; Weili Ge and Sarah E. McVay, "On the Disclosure of Material Weaknesses in Internal Control after the Sarbanes-Oxley Act," *Accounting Horizons* 19, no. 3 (September 2005):123.

49. Securities and Exchange Act of 1934, s 12(g)(5).

50. See Engel et al., "The Sarbanes-Oxley Act and Firms' Going-Private Decisions" (also finding more favorable share price reaction to going private in firms with high inside ownership, which may have had relatively low benefits from being public, and therefore larger net gains from going private); Christian Leuz, Alexander J. Triantis, and Tracy Yue Wang, "Why Do Firms Go Dark? Causes and Economic Consequences of Voluntary SEC Deregistrations," Social Science Research Network Working Paper Series, AFA 2006 Boston Meetings Paper, 2004, http://papers.ssrn.com/sol3/papers.cfm?abstract_id=592421 (accessed March 21, 2006).

51. Ehud Kamar, Pinar Karaca-Mandic, and Eric Talley, "Going-Private Decisions and the Sarbanes-Oxley Act of 2002: A Cross-Country Analysis," November 2005, http://www.law.ucla.edu/docs/talley_012306.pdf (accessed April 3, 2006).

52. For a debate on this issue, see Victor Fleischer, "Is SOX Leading More Firms to Go Private?" January 24, 2006, *Conglomerate*, http://www.theconglomerate.org/2006/01/is_sox_leading_.html (accessed April 3, 2006), and Larry E. Ribstein, "Who Cares about the Disappearing Small Public Firms?" *Ideoblog*, January 24, 2006, http://busmovie.typepad.com/ideoblog/2006/ 01/who_cares_about.html (accessed April 3, 2006).

53. See Leuz et al., "Why Do Firms Go Dark?"; Engel et al., "The Sarbanes-Oxley Act and Firms' Going-Private Decisions"; Carney, "The Costs of Being Public"; Andras Marosi and Nadia Ziad Massoud, "Why Do Firms Go Dark?" Social Science Research Network Working Paper Series, November 2004, http://papers.ssrn.com/sol3/papers.cfm?abstract_id=570421 (accessed April 12, 2006).

54. See Leuz et al., "Why Do Firms Go Dark?"; Marosi and Massoud, "Why Do Firms Go Dark?"

55. Leuz et al., "Why Do Firms Go Dark?"

56. See Rick Antle, Elizabeth A. Gordon, Ganapathi Narayanamoorthy, and Ling Zhou, "The Joint Determination of Audit Fees, Non-Audit Fees,

and Abnormal Accruals," Social Science Research Network Working Paper Series, Working Paper No. AC-15, Yale School of Management, June 14, 2002 (showing that audit firms' provision of nonaudit services did not affect the incidence of abnormal accruals), http://papers.ssrn.com/paper.taf ?abstract_id=318943 (accessed March 21, 2006).

57. As to the interrelation between law and trust, see Larry E. Ribstein, "Law v. Trust," *Boston University Law Review* 81, no. 3 (June 2001): 553–90.

58. See, for example, Bruno S. Frey, *Not Just for the Money* (Cheltenham, U.K., and Brookfield, Vt.: Edward Elgar, 1997), 7–8.

59. Richard W. Painter, "Lawyers' Rules, Auditors' Rules and the Psychology of Concealment," *Minnesota Law Review* 84, no. 6 (June 2000): 1399–1438; Jeffrey J. Rachlinski, "Gains, Losses, and the Psychology of Litigation," *Southern California Law Review* 70, no. 1 (November 1996): 113–86.

60. As for insurance, the firm and the shareholders are probably in a better position to monitor executives than the insurer. This may explain why directors' and officers' liability insurance became costlier and scarcer after Enron and WorldCom increased the liability threat and, thus, the burden on insurers relative to shareholders. See Christopher Oster, "Directors' Insurance Fees Get Fatter," *Wall Street Journal*, July 12, 2002, C1 (discussing the large rise in premiums and deductibles); Christopher Oster, "Insurers Expected to Try to Deny WorldCom Officers' Coverage," *Wall Street Journal*, July 1, 2002, C14 (noting that "the recent rash of earnings restatements and accounting problems has driven up rates for D&O policies"). Indemnification just throws the risk back on the corporation and the shareholders, where it belonged in the first place.

61. See Gerald J. Lobo and Jian Zhou, "Did Conservatism in Financial Reporting Increase after the Sarbanes-Oxley Act? Initial Evidence," *Accounting Horizons* 20, no. 1 (March 2006): 57–73 (showing an increase in conservatism in financial reporting following SOX, including reporting lower discretionary accruals, incorporating losses more quickly than gains in reporting income).

62. Bhagat and Romano, "Event Studies and the Law," 409 (reviewing studies).

63. See Paul Rosenzweig, "The Over-Criminalization of Social and Economic Conduct," Heritage Foundation Legal Memorandum No. 7, http://www.heritage.org/Research/LegalIssues/lm7.cfm. (accessed April 3, 2006).

64. SEC commissioner Paul S. Atkins summarizes the problem:

> Before people will rationalize their approach to the internal control process, both the SEC and the PCAOB will have to give people comfort that we will actually allow people to use their professional judgment and that they will not be second-guessed. Both the SEC and the PCAOB recently issued guidance on these issues. Both sets of guidance acknowledged that more needs to be done in this area and that the current approach was too granular, was not risk-based and did not employ a top-down strategy.

Remarks before the SIA Leadership Luncheon, San Francisco, June 8, 2005, http://www.sec.gov/news/speech/spch060805psa.htm (accessed April 3, 2006).

65. See pp. 41–42

66. At least in jury trials, this dynamic is further affected by prosecutors' ability to take advantage of what has been called criminal defendants' "ambiguity aversion": While prosecutors are repeat players whose decision depends on the known overall conviction rate, defendants only care about their individual cases, where the prospects are ambiguous. See Alex Stein and Uzi Segal, "Ambiguity Aversion and the Criminal Process," *Notre Dame Law Review* 81, no. 4 (2006, forthcoming), available at http://papers.ssrn.com/paper.taf?abstract_id=846044 (accessed March 21, 2006).

67. U.S. Department of Justice, Office of the Deputy Attorney General, "Memorandum on Principles of Federal Prosecution of Business Organizations," January 20, 2003, http://www.usdoj.gov/dag/cftf/corporate _guidelines.htm (accessed March 29, 2006).

68. See John Hasnas, "Department of Coercion."

69. See ABA Task Force on Attorney-Client Privilege, "Recommendation 111," Task Force Releases Report and Recommendation to the ABA House of Delegates, August 9, 2005, http://www.abanet.org/buslaw/attorneyclient/ materials/hod/recommendation_adopted.pdf (accessed March 22, 2006).

70. See Antle et al., "The Joint Determination of Audit Fees."

71. The evidence on the value of this restriction is far from convincing. Romano showed that fifteen of twenty-five studies on the effect of nonaudit services on audit quality reports demonstrated no connection between the two, one found no connection for big-five accounting firms, and three found that nonaudit services improved audit quality. Testing of other relevant factors undercuts other surveys' findings that nonaudit services

affect quality. See Romano, "The Sarbanes-Oxley Act and the Making of Quack Corporate Governance," 1535–37. There is also evidence of negative market reaction to the restriction on provision of nonaudit services. See Zabihollah Rezaee and Pankaj K. Jain, "The Sarbanes-Oxley Act of 2002 and Security Market Behavior: Early Evidence," Social Science Research Network Working Paper Series, March 22, 2004, http://papers.ssrn.com/sol3/papers.cfm?abstract_id=498083 (accessed March 21, 2006).

72. See Lynnley Browning, "Sorry, the Auditor Said, But We Want a Divorce," New York Times, February 6, 2005, sec. 3, p. 5, col. 1.

73. See James C. Spindler, "Conflict or Credibility: Analyst Conflicts of Interest and the Market for Underwriting Business," Social Science Research Network Working Paper Series, Olin Working Paper No. 215, University of Chicago Law School, John M. Olin Program in Law and Economics, http://papers.ssrn.com/sol3/papers.cfm?abstract_id=564381 (accessed March 21, 2006).

74. Santa Fe Industries Inc. v. Green, 430 U.S. 462 (1977).

75. See David A. Skeel Jr., "Rethinking the Line Between Corporate Law and Corporate Bankruptcy," Texas Law Review 72, no. 3 (February 1994): 471–558 (arguing that the federal law of corporate bankruptcy discourages both state and federal resolution of issues that lie in the boundary between bankruptcy and state law).

76. See chapter 4, pp. 33–35.

77. Chandler and Strine, "The New Federalism."

78. In re Caremark International Inc. Derivative Litigation, 698 A.2d 959 (Del. Ch. 1996).

79. Chandler and Strine, "The New Federalism," 979–80.

80. Newcastle Partners L.P. v. Vesta Insurance Group Inc., 887 A.2d 957 (Del. Ch. 2005). See the discussion in Larry E. Ribstein, "A Chicken Game in Delaware," Ideoblog, November 19, 2005, http://busmovie.typepad.com/ ideoblog/2005/11/a_chicken_game_.html (accessed April 3, 2006).

81. Myron Steele, "Sarbox and De," NYU Journal of Law and Liberty Blog, October 27, 2005, http://www.nyujll.org/blog/index.php?paged=3 (accessed April 3, 2006).

82. Leo E. Strine Jr., "Derivative Impact? Some Early Reflections on Corporate Law Implications of the Enron Debacle," Business Lawyer 57, no. 4 (August 2002): 1372.

83. Renee M. Jones, "Rethinking Corporate Federalism in the Era of Corporate Reform," Journal of Corporation Law 29, no. 3 (Spring 2004): 625–64.

84. See Lisa M. Fairfax, "Sarbanes-Oxley, Corporate Federalism, and the Declining Significance of Federal Reforms on State Director Independence Standards," *Ohio Northern University Law Review* 31, no. 3 (2005): 381–416.

85. See *Brehm v. Eisner*, 747 A. 2d 244 (Del. 2000).

86. *In re Walt Disney Company Derivative Litigation*, 825 A.2d 275 (Del. Ch., 2003).

87. *In re Walt Disney Company Derivative Litigation* (Del. Ch., August 9, 2005), 2005 WL 1875804.

88. See Roe, "Delaware's Competition," 643 (commenting after the chancellor's 2003 opinion that "the difficulty here is to sort out whether its abrupt shift was due primarily to the federal gravitational pull, to the dynamics of the litigation, or to the state's direct perception of the underlying corporate problems").

89. See Chandler and Strine, "The New Federalism," 992.

90. Ibid., 998.

91. Roberta Romano, *The Genius of American Corporate Law*.

92. 17 CFR §240.10A-3(e)(1)(i).

93. See Mara Faccio and Larry Lang, "The Ultimate Ownership of Western European Corporations," *Journal of Financial Economics* 65, no. 3 (September 2002): 365–95.

94. Aktiengesetz §119 I Nr. 5; HGB §318 I.

95. 17 CFR §78j-1(m)(3).

96. See Lawrence A. Cunningham, "From Convergence to Comity in Corporate Law: Lessons from the Inauspicious Case of SOX," *International Journal of Disclosure and Governance* 1, no. 3 (June 2004): 269–98.

97. See David Reilly and Sarah Nassauer, "Street Sleuth, Tip-Line Bind: Follow the Law In U.S. or EU?" *Wall Street Journal*, September 6, 2005, C1, http://online.wsj.com/article/0,,SB112596782625632302,00.html?mod=todays_us_money_and_investing (accessed April 3, 2006).

98. See Erin Marks, "The Sarbanes-Oxley Act: Costs and Tradeoffs Relating to International Application and Convergence," *Research in Accounting Regulation* 17 (2004), Social Science Research Network Accepted Paper Series, http://papers.ssrn.com/sol3/papers.cfm?abstract_id=499403 (accessed March 21, 2006); Ribstein, "Cross-Listing and Regulatory Competition."

99. See Craig Karmin and Aaron Lucchetti, "New York Loses Edge in Snagging Foreign Listings," *Wall Street Journal*, January 26, 2006, C1, http://online.wsj.com/article/SB113824819390656771.html?mod=todays_us_money_and_investing (accessed April 3, 2006).

100. See Craig Karmin, "London Calling," *Wall Street Journal*, December 23, 2005 C1, http://online.wsj.com/article/SB113530126767530086-search.html?KEYWORDS=london+calling&COLLECTION=wsjie/6month/ (accessed April 3, 2006).

101. See Michael A. Perino, "American Corporate Reform Abroad: Sarbanes-Oxley and the Foreign Private Issuer," *European Business Organization Law Review* 4, no. 3 (October 2003): 213–44.

102. Kate Litvak, "The Effect of the Sarbanes-Oxley Act on Non-US Companies Cross-Listed in the US," Social Science Research Network Working Paper Series, Law and Economics Research Paper No. 55, University of Texas Law School, December 22, 2005, http://papers.ssrn.com/sol3/papers.cfm?abstract_id=876624 (accessed March 21, 2006).

103. For the initial outcry, see the comments by representatives of foreign firms in response to the SEC's rulemaking on the audit committee requirements. These comments are collected at http://www.sec.gov/rules/proposed/s70203.shtml, and summarized at http://www.sec.gov/rules/extra/s70203summary.htm#P1121_88452 (accessed April 3, 2006).

104. See Anna Snider, "Going SOX-less," *California Lawyer*, October 2004, 37; Floyd H. Norris, "European Companies Push for Relief from U.S. Security Laws," *International Herald Tribune*, February 12, 2004, http://www.iht.com/articles/2004/02/12/comply_ed3_.php (accessed April 3, 2006).

105. 17 CFR §240.10A-3.

106. 17 CFR §240.10A-3(c)(3).

107. See Securities and Exchange Commission, "Proposed Rules: Insider Trades During Pension Fund Blackout Periods," November 6, 2002, 17 CFR §§240, 245 and 249 [Release 34-46778; IC-25795; File No. S7-44-02], http://www.sec.gov/rules/proposed/34-46778.htm (accessed April 3, 2006).

108. See "Implementation of Standards of Professional Conduct for Attorneys," Release 33-8185, 17 CFR 205.2(j) (defining "non-appearing foreign attorney"), August 5, 2003, http://www.sec.gov/rules/final/33-8185.htm (accessed April 3, 2006).

109. SEC Release 33-8545.

Chapter 5: The Litigation Time Bomb

1. See SEC Release 33-8238.

2. See Sarbanes-Oxley Act §3(b)(1), 15 U.S.C. §7202.

3. SEC Litigation Release 18044 (March 20, 2003). The certification was pursuant to SEC Order 4-460, Order Requiring the Filing of Sworn

Statements Pursuant to §21(a)(1) of the Securities Exchange Act of 1934 (June 27, 2002). A court has already upheld the constitutionality of section 906 in connection with this case. *U.S. v. Scrushy*, 2004 WL 2713262 (N.D. Ala. 2004).

4. It is interesting to speculate how these provisions and rules might have been applied to the frauds at Enron and other companies that provided the impetus for SOX. Many of these cases involved bad accounting by underlings in the company for largely correct underlying data. For example, Xerox accelerated revenues from long-term equipment leases, Qwest and Global Crossing manipulated revenues and expenses on sales of fiber optic capacity, and, most notoriously, WorldCom blatantly misstated billions in current expenses the company incurred to use transmission networks as capital expenditures. Some cases, like Sunbeam, involved false data—in that case, phony sales and rebates. This is reminiscent of one of the biggest frauds of all, Equity Funding, in which managers and employees simply manufactured life insurance policies.

Consider also cases where the impropriety of the accounting depends on complex background facts. For example, some of Enron's off-balance-sheet, special-purpose entities should have been on the balance sheet under applicable accounting rules because they had outside (non-Enron) equity of less than three percent of total capital. Andrew Fastow, Enron's chief financial officer, told the Enron board that the entities did have the requisite outside equity, but this was not true. As it happened, he never gave the board the specifics. SOX will now clearly require senior executives to get the specifics—but what if the Fastow of the future Enron lies or fabricates documents? More problematically, what if there is no background documentation? In the notorious Nigerian Barge case, Merrill Lynch brokers face jail for assisting in a transaction that was purportedly a purchase of barges from Enron but was allegedly not a legitimate sale because of an informal promise by Enron to buy the barges back. The court had to rely on hearsay as to the side deal.

A similar case arose recently in which the inside counsel of a Siemens subsidiary was indicted for preparing a transaction for a minority-owned joint venture that was allegedly not really a joint venture. The indictment quotes an email that established the absence of the requisite profit-sharing arrangement. It says that the Siemens subsidiary "relied on Roth [the inside counsel] to ensure legal compliance with the applicable ordinances." *U.S. v. Faust Villazan*, Superseding Indictment, 05 CR 792 (N.D. Ill. 2006), para. 11.

5. Harvey L. Pitt, "Commentary, Trials and Tribulations of Enron and S-Ox," Forbes.com, January 23, 2006, http://www.forbes.com/columnists/2006/01/20/enron-sarbox-pitt-commentary-cx_hlp_0123harveypitt.html (accessed April 3, 2006).

6. For example, under what circumstances might the executives of Siemens be liable under SOX in the situation just discussed for failing to have internal controls that would have caught the fact that the enterprise might not have been a joint venture?

7. Pitt, "Commentary, Trials and Tribulations."

8. See Chandler and Strine, "The New Federalism," 987.

9. See ibid., 987n90 (noting the qualification in Del. Code. Ann. Tit. 8, §102(b)(7)(ii) for knowing violation of law). To the extent that federal law compels directors to do what Delaware law permits or requires, state courts might be forced to align state with federal standards. This was the issue that was narrowly avoided in the *Vesta* case, discussed on p. 68.

10. See Mitu Gulati, Jeffrey J. Rachlinski, and Donald C. Langevoort, "Fraud by Hindsight," *Northwestern University Law Review* 98, no. 3 (2004): 773–826.

11. See Kenneth M. Lehn, "Private Insecurities," *Wall Street Journal*, February 15, 2006, A16, http://online.wsj.com/article/SB11399676486537 4191.html?mod=todays_us_opinion (accessed April 3, 2006).

12. See *Dura Pharmaceuticals Inc. v. Broudo*, 125 S.Ct. 1627 (2005) (holding that allegations of price inflation at the time of purchase were insufficient and implying that plaintiff must also allege a market adjustment following a corrective disclosure).

13. See Larry E. Ribstein, "Fraud on a Noisy Market," *Lewis & Clark Law Review* 10, no. 1 (2006): 137–68.

14. See Richard A. Booth, "Who Should Recover What in a Securities Fraud Class Action?" Social Science Research Network Working Paper Series, University of Maryland Legal Studies Research Paper No. 2005-32, February 2005, http://papers.ssrn.com/sol3/papers.cfm?abstract_id=683197 (accessed March 21, 2006).

Chapter 6: The Bottom Line: Has SOX Been Worth It?

1. See Romano, "The Sarbanes-Oxley Act and the Making of Quack Corporate Governance," 1541–43.

2. See Zhang, "Economic Consequences of the Sarbanes-Oxley Act."

3. Haidan Li, Morton Pincus, and Sonja O. Rego, "Market Reaction to Events Surrounding the Sarbanes-Oxley Act of 2002," Social Science Research Network Working Paper Series, January 11, 2006, http://papers .ssrn.com/sol3/papers.cfm?abstract_id=475163 (accessed March 21, 2006).

4. Vidhi Chhaochharia and Yaniv Grinstein, "Corporate Governance and Firm Value—The Impact of the 2002 Governance Rules," June 2004, Social

Science Research Network Working Paper Series, AFA 2006 Boston Meetings Paper, http://papers.ssrn.com/sol3/papers.cfm?abstract_id=556990 (accessed March 21, 2006).

5. See Rezaee and Jain, "Sarbanes-Oxley Act of 2002 and Security Market Behavior."

6. See Paul A. Griffin and David H. Lont, "Taking the Oath: Investor Response to SEC Certification," November 19, 2003, Social Science Research Network Working Paper Series (showing more positive reaction for firms with prior securities litigation), http://papers.ssrn.com/paper.taf?abstract_id=477586 (accessed March 21, 2006); Beverly Hirtle, "Stock Market Reaction to Financial Statement Certification by Bank Holding Company CEOs," Social Science Research Network Working Paper Series, FRB of New York Staff Report No. 170, July 2003 (for bank holding companies that certified prior to the rule's compliance deadline, showing that the effect on share prices was correlated with the opacity of the firm's earnings), http://papers.ssrn.com/sol3/papers.cfm?abstract_id=425002 (accessed March 21, 2006).

7. Uptal Bhattacharya, Peter Groznik, and Bruce Haslem, "Is CEO Certification Credible?" *Regulation* 26, no. 3 (Fall 2003): 8–10, available at http://papers.ssrn.com/paper.taf?abstract_id=511122 (accessed April 3, 2006).

8. See Romano, "The Sarbanes-Oxley Act and the Making of Quack Corporate Governance," 1542.

9. See Maria Ogneva, Kannan Raghunandan, and K. R. Subramanyam, "Internal Control Weakness and Cost of Equity: Evidence from SOX Section 404 Certifications," Social Science Research Network Working Paper Series, AAA 2006 Financial Accounting and Reporting Section (FARS) Meeting Paper, October 2005, http://ssrn.com/abstract=766104 (accessed March 21, 2006).

10. See Editorial, "Overseeing Refco," *Wall Street Journal*, October 17, 2005, A18, http://online.wsj.com/article/SB112950980774970305.html?mod=todays_us_opinion (accessed April 3, 2006); Deborah Solomon and Michael Shroeder, "How Refco Fell Through Regulatory Cracks," *Wall Street Journal*, October 18, 2005, A18, http://online.wsj.com/article/SB112959398166971354.html?mod=todays_us_page_one (accessed April 3, 2006).

11. See Laing, "The Bear that Roared."

12. See generally, Ribstein, "Fraud on a Noisy Market."

Chapter 7: Immediate Policy Implications

1. See Chris Evans, "Directors Call for Sarbanes-Oxley Repeal," *Accountancy Age*, February 23, 2006, http://www.accountancyage.com/accountancyage/news/2150885/sarbanes-story (accessed April 3, 2006).

2. See introduction, p. 6. For further analysis, see Nagy, "Playing Peeka-boo With Constitutional Law."

3. The SEC is already considering some of these changes, particularly including the forthcoming recommendations of its Advisory Committee on Smaller Public Companies; see SEC Advisory Committee, "Final Report."

4. Ibid., 44n96, argues that the SEC has authority to adopt exemptions for small firms under the Securities and Exchange Act, section 36(a)(1) and SOX section 3(a). However, the former section does not even apply to SOX section 404, which is not part of the Exchange Act, while the latter provides only for rules "in furtherance of this Act," which, arguably, would not include a broad exemption. See William Sjostrom, "Can the SEC Exempt Small Companies from Sarbanes-Oxley 404?" (part 2), *Truth on the Market*, February 27, 2006, http://www.truthonthemarket.com/2006/02/27/can-the-sec-exempt-small-companies-from-sarbanes-oxley-404-part-2/.

5. 119 Stat. 4, http://files.findlaw.com/news.findlaw.com/hdocs/docs/clssactns/cafa05.pdf (accessed April 2, 2006).

6. See p. 80, n. 12.

7. 125 S.Ct., 1634.

8. See, generally, Easterbrook and Fischel, *Economic Structure of Corporate Law*, chapter 11.

9. See SEC rule 14a-8.

10. The SEC's Advisory Committee on Smaller Public Companies is considering a broad opt-in proposal for smaller firms; see SEC Advisory Committee, "Final Report," 40–42.

11. See chapter 3, p. 35.

12. See SEC rules 3b-4(b) and 3b-4(c).

13. See Ribstein, "Cross-Listing and Regulatory Competition."

14. See chapter 1, p. 14.

Chapter 8: The Future: Regulatory Hubris or Greater Humility?

1. James Fanto, "Paternalistic Regulation of Public Company Management: Lessons from Bank Regulation," January 4, 2006, Social Science Research Network Working Paper Series, Brooklyn Law School Legal Studies Paper No. 49, http://papers.ssrn.com/sol3/papers.cfm?abstract_id=873667 (accessed March 21, 2006). For a critique, see Larry E. Ribstein, "Business Corporations as Banks: The Next Step in Corporate Governance Reform?" *Ideoblog*, January 21, 2006, http://busmovie.typepad.com/ideoblog/2006/01/business_corpor.html (accessed April 3, 2006).

2. Ohio e-CPA Weekly, "Oxley Says Some SOX Reforms 'Excessive'" (quoting *Financial Times*), http://www.ohioscpa.com/publications/ohiocpa/default.asp?article=3505-1 (accessed April 3, 2006).

3. See Congressional Research Service, Library of Congress, "USA Patriot Act Sunset: Provisions that Expire on December 31, 2005," http://fpc.state.gov/documents/organization/34499.pdf (accessed April 3, 2006).

4. See Stephen Choi, "Market Lessons for Gatekeepers," *Northwestern University Law Review* 92, no. 3 (1998): 916–66.

5. Romano, "The Sarbanes-Oxley Act and the Making of Quack Corporate Governance," 1595–97, also discusses the possibility of optional regulation.

6. It may be necessary to adjust disclosure requirements to be sure they produce meaningful information. See Sridhar Arcot and Valentina Giulia Bruno, "In Letter But Not in Spirit: An Analysis of Corporate Governance in the UK," Social Science Research Network Working Paper Series, May 26, 2005, http://papers.ssrn.com/paper.taf?abstract_id=819784 (accessed March 21, 2006) (showing that firms increasingly are complying with the "comply or explain" regulations in the United Kingdom, but often using standard explanations for noncompliance).

7. See chapter 3.

8. See Lawrence A. Cunningham, *Outsmarting the Smart Money* (New York: McGraw-Hill, 2002), 181–200; Lawrence A. Cunningham, "Behavioral Finance and Investor Governance," *Washington and Lee Law Review* 59, no. 3 (Summer 2003): 767–838.

9. The SEC has already moved in this direction. See Securities Exchange Commission, "Analyzing Analyst Recommendations" (suggesting that investors note potential conflicts inherent in analyst recommendations), http://www.sec.gov/investor/pubs/analysts.htm (accessed April 3, 2006).

10. See Donald C. Langevoort, "Managing the 'Expectations Gap' in Investor Protection: The SEC and the Post-Enron Reform Agenda," *Villanova Law Review* 48, no. 4 (2003): 1139–66 (arguing that the SEC must try "to persuade investors that the issuers are honest enough to justify broad and confident public participation without committing its own version of a fraud on the market"); see also Donald C. Langevoort, "Taming the Animal Spirits of the Stock Markets: A Behavioral Approach to Securities Regulation," *Northwestern University Law Review* 97, no. 1 (2002–3): 151 (discussing the "myth" of desirability of encouraging trading by the retail investor); Henry T. C. Hu, "Faith and Magic: Investor Beliefs and Government Neutrality," *Texas Law Review* 78, no. 4 (2000): 883 (noting that government intervention "has led many investors to believe that [the Federal Reserve] can and would prevent a stock market crash").

11. Securities and Exchange Commission, "Selective Disclosure and Insider Trading," Exchange Act Release 33-7881, August 15, 2000, http://www.sec.gov/rules/final/33-7881.htm (accessed April 7, 2006).

12. See Laura S. Unger (commissioner), "SEC Special Study: Regulation Fair Disclosure Revisited," December 2001, http://www.sec.gov/news/studies/regfdstudy.htm (accessed April 3, 2006).

13. See Anwer S. Ahmed and Richard A. Schneible Jr., "Did Regulation Fair Disclosure Level the Playing Field? Evidence from an Analysis of Changes in Trading Volume and Stock Price Reactions to Earnings Announcements," Social Science Research Network Working Paper Series, January 22, 2004, http://papers.ssrn.com/paper.taf?abstract_id=498002 (accessed March 21, 2006).

14. Anup Agrawal, Sahiba Chadha, and Mark A. Chen, "Who is Afraid of Reg FD? The Behavior and Performance of Sell-Side Analysts Following the SEC's Fair Disclosure Rules," Social Science Research Network Working Paper Series, paper presented at AFA 2003 Washington, D.C., meetings, October 2002, http://papers.ssrn.com/sol3/papers.cfm?abstract_id=738685 (March 21, 2006).

15. See David D. Haddock and Jonathan R. Macey, "A Coasian Model of Insider Trading," *Northwestern University Law Review* 80, no. 6 (1986): 1449–72.

About the Authors

Henry N. Butler is the James Farley Professor of Economics, Argyros School of Business and Economics, Chapman University. He earned his B.A. in economics from the University of Richmond, M.A. and Ph.D. in economics from Virginia Tech, and J.D. from the University of Miami. His research interests include corporate governance, federalism, and law and economics. He recently completed the second edition of his casebook, *Economics Analysis for Lawyers* (co-authored with Christopher Drahozal). He has devoted a substantial amount of his career to improving our nation's judiciary through various judicial education programs. He is currently Director of the Judicial Education Program offered by the AEI-Brookings Joint Center for Regulatory Studies.

Larry E. Ribstein is the Richard and Marie Corman Professor of Law, University of Illinois College of Law. He earned his J.D. at the University of Chicago Law School, and his A.B. at Johns Hopkins University. Ribstein is a scholar in the areas of unincorporated business entities, partnerships, and limited liability companies, corporate and securities law, bankruptcy, and choice of law. He is the author of two casebooks on business associations, the leading multivolume treatises on partnership law and on limited liability companies, and has served as an editor of the *Supreme Court Economic Review*.

Index

Accounting lobby, 13–14
Adelphia, 9
Advisory Committee on Smaller Public Companies (SEC), 47, 91–92
Agency theory, 23–25
Akerlof, George, 30
American Bar Association, 17, 56, 63
AMR Research, 40
Ancillary services by auditors, 63–64
Arthur Andersen, 8, 42–43, 63
Attestation, *see* Certification
Attorneys, *see* Lawyers
Audit committees (board), 21, 42–43, 45–46, 70–71, 100
Auditors, 21, 39–43, 56, 63–64, 101
Audit standard 2, 40

Ballmer, Steve, 8
Barnard, Jayne, 18, 46
Berle, Adolf, 1, 23
Blackmail, litigation, potential for, 79–81
Blue Chip Stamps, 87
Bush, George W., 9, 47, 83
    and Harken Energy stock, 15–16, 18–19

Business community
    future posture on regulation, 95–96
    lack of effective opposition to SOX passage, 11–16
Business judgment rule, 24–25
Business Roundtable, 12

Capital market forces, alternatives to SOX, 27–32
Cary, William, 33
Certification of internal controls disclosure, 38–40, 49, 77, 97
Chamber of Commerce, U.S., 12
Chandler, William B. III, 66–67, 69–70
Class Action Fairness Act (2005), 87
Cloture on SOX, 15–17
Congress
    and possible changes or repeal of SOX, 6, 42, 46–47, 86–93, 96–97, 102
    and process of passing SOX, 3, 7–16, 20, 49–50, 88
Consultant services, 64
Consulting industry, 13
Corporate law, *see* State corporate law

131